William Allan, Association Lee Memorial

Ceremonies connected with the inauguration of the mausoleum

William Allan, Association Lee Memorial

Ceremonies connected with the inauguration of the mausoleum

ISBN/EAN: 9783337224981

Printed in Europe, USA, Canada, Australia, Japan

Cover: Foto ©ninafisch / pixelio.de

More available books at **www.hansebooks.com**

CEREMONIES

CONNECTED WITH

THE INAUGURATION OF THE MAUSOLEUM AND THE UNVEILING
OF THE RECUMBENT FIGURE

OF

GENERAL ROBERT EDWARD LEE,

AT

WASHINGTON AND LEE UNIVERSITY,

LEXINGTON, VA., JUNE 28, 1883.

ORATION OF JOHN W. DANIEL, LL. D.

HISTORICAL SKETCH

OF THE

LEE MEMORIAL ASSOCIATION.

LYNCHBURG, VA.:
J. P. BELL & CO., PRINTERS,
1883.

HISTORICAL SKETCH
OF THE
LEE MEMORIAL ASSOCIATION,
BY
W. ALLAN.
A Member of the Executive Committee.

GENERAL ROBERT EDWARD LEE was prostrated by his last illness on September 28, 1870. He died two weeks later, on the morning of October 12. On October 15 he was buried beneath the chapel of Washington College, now Washington and Lee University, Lexington, Virginia. This place was selected by Mrs. Lee after the authorities of the College had placed at her disposal any part of the grounds she might prefer. The day, though full of the glory of autumn, was the most mournful in the annals of Lexington. A vast concourse, comprising the entire population of the town and the vicinity, with delegations from other places, followed, with sadness and tears, the remains of General Lee to the tomb. The funeral services were conducted by the Rev. W. N. Pendleton, D. D., (late Brigadier General and Chief of Artillery of the Army of Northern Virginia,) the rector of Grace Episcopal Church, of which General Lee was a member. The body was deposited in a vault prepared for the purpose.

On the day of the funeral a large number of ex-Confederate soldiers assembled in the court-house at Lexington, and after giving expression to the love and veneration of the South for General Lee, and to the sorrow at his death, resolved to take steps to erect a monument in honor of their great leader. They felt that even in the midst of poverty and disaster, no labor could be more grateful, no duty more sacred, than that of making manifest to the future, in some enduring way, the love and admiration of his countrymen for the character and genius of Robert E. Lee.

At this meeting was formed the LEE MEMORIAL ASSOCIATION, and the following were appointed an Executive Committee to carry into effect the objects of the Association:

Gen. W. N. Pendleton, Chief Artillery, A. N. V.
Capt. J. J. White, Liberty Hall Vols., 4th Va. Reg't.
Col. J. K. Edmondson, 27th Va. Reg't.
Col. W. Preston Johnston, Staff of President Davis.
Capt. A. Graham, Rockbridge Artillery.
Maj. Jas. B. Dorman, C. S. A.
Lt.-Col. W. Allan, Chief Ord. Officer, 2nd Corps, A. N. V.
Capt. J. C. Boude, 27th Va. Reg't.
Capt. C. A. Davidson, 1st Va. Battalion.
Lt.-Col. Wm. M. McLaughlin, Artillery, C. S. A.
Lt.-Col. J. W. Massie, 51st Va. Reg't.
W. A. Anderson, Liberty Hall Vols., 4th Va. Reg't.

This Committee met October 24, 1870, at the office of Capt. C. A. Davidson, and organized by electing Gen. W. N. Pendleton as chairman, and Capt. Charles A. Davidson as secretary. The Committee, in accordance with the duties entrusted to it, then elected the following officers of the Lee Memorial Association:

President—Gen. Jno. C. Breckinridge, of Kentucky.
Vice-Pres't-at-Large—Gen. Jos. E. Johnston, of Virginia.
Vice-Pres'ts from Virginia, { Gen. Jubal A. Early, Col. Walter H. Taylor.
Vice-Pres't from Louisiana, Gen. P. G. T. Beauregard.
" " " N. Carolina, Gen. D. H. Hill.
" " " S. Carolina, Gen. Wade Hampton.
" " " Georgia, Gen. John B. Gordon.
" " " Alabama, Gen. W. J. Hardee.
" " " Mississippi, Gen. S. D. Lee.
" " " Tennessee, R. S. Ewell.
" " " Texas, Gen. Jno. B. Hood.
" " " Maryland, Gen. I. R. Trimble.
" " " Missouri, Gen. J. S. Marmaduke.
" " " Arkansas, Gen. J. C. Tappan.
Treasurer, C. M. Figgat, Esq., Cashier Bank of Lexington, Va.

A committee was appointed to prepare an address for publication, setting forth the purposes of the Association, and another committee was instructed to draw up a charter, and to submit it to the Legislature of Virginia for enactment.

Mrs. Mary Custis Lee was requested by the Executive Committee to indicate her preference in regard to the monument to be erected by the Association, and at her suggestion, Mr. Ed. V. Valentine, the distinguished Virginian sculptor, was sent for. Mr. Valentine had, the preceding summer, modeled a bust of General Lee from life, which was considered an admirable work of art. Mrs. Lee, after examining a number of drawings and photographs of celebrated works of art, suggested, as a suitable design for the monument, a recumbent figure of General Lee lying asleep upon the field of battle. The design was suggested to her by Ranch's figure of Louise of Prussia in the mausoleum at Charlottenburg. This figure of Lee, somewhat above life size, was to be placed upon a sarcophagus suitably inscribed and decorated. The whole was to be of white marble and was designed to be placed over the remains of General Lee.

The suggestions of Mrs. Lee, both as to the monument and as to the artist, having been cordially adopted by the Association, Mr. Valentine was, on November 24, 1870, requested to "prepare a design for the tomb of Gen. R. E. Lee, proposed to be erected, and an estimate of the probable cost of the same." Measures were also taken for collecting from the admirers of General Lee, the funds needed for erecting the monument. Liberal responses were received from a number of sources, among which was a donation of $1000 from W. W. Corcoran, Esq., of Washington, and the Executive Committee became satisfied that the means needed for the work could be obtained.

On June 23, 1871, Mr. Valentine, having completed a model of the proposed figure and sarcophagus, appeared before the Executive Committee and submitted it together with an estimate of cost. This latter amounted to $15,000. The model was approved and accepted, and Mr. Valentine was commissioned to go on with the work.

By the fall of 1872 Mr. Valentine had completed the cast of the monument in plaster and was ready to put it into marble. Some $5,000 had up to this time been contributed to the Association, and active steps were now taken to collect the remainder of the sum needed to secure the completion of the figure. The Association of the Army of Northern Virginia, at its meeting in Richmond, October 31, 1872, resolved:

"That the sarcophagus now in course of preparation by our Virginian artist, Valentine, to be placed over the tomb of Lee, at Lexington, commends itself to especial favor as promising, from the beauty of the design, and the skill of the sculptor, to be a worthy memorial of our departed chief.

"That for the purpose of assuring and expediting the completion of this noble work of art, to be placed, as a fitting token of a whole people's love and homage, above the ashes of their dead hero, we recommend to the ladies of the South to hold memorial meetings on the next anniversary of the birth of Gen. R. E. Lee, and to take such measures as shall to them seem best for collecting money on that day to be specially appropriated to the decoration of his tomb by the erection of the sarcophagus."

The Memorial Association in an address united their voice with that of the Association of the A. N. V.

The ladies of Lexington promptly responded by having a fair and a cantata in the winter of 1872–'3, the proceeds of which, amounting to over $800, were turned over to the Association. This sum was still further increased by private subscriptions. The example thus set was followed in many other places. On the 20th January, 1873, contributions were made in a number of Southern cities and towns to the object of the Association. In Savannah, Gen. Hampton, by invitation, delivered a lecture upon Gen. Lee, which added over $500 to the funds of the Association. The ladies of Leesburg, Va., of Alexandria, Va., and of Palmyra, Missouri, sent handsome contributions. Similar responses came from many other places. During the spring and summer contributions continued to come in. Among these was a liberal donation of $500 from W. H.

McLellan, Esq., of New Orleans. Admirers of Gen. Lee abroad also contributed liberally. Mr. W. T. McCauslane, of Glasgow, Scotland, took particular interest in the matter, and through his efforts nearly $700 were added to the funds of the Association. A considerable sum was realized from a steel engraving of Gen. Lee published by Bostwick & Co., of Cincinnati, and sold under the authority of the Association; also, from the sale of "Personal Reminiscences of Gen. Lee" by Rev. J. W. Jones, D. D., a part of the proceeds of which book were turned over to the Executive Committee.

An act incorporating the Association had been passed by the Virginia Legislature and approved January 14, 1871. By this it was enacted, "That Wm. N. Pendleton, F. W. M. Holliday, C. S. Venable, J. W. Massie, Charles A. Davidson, Wm. McLaughlin, J. B. Dorman, Wm. Allan, Wm. P. Johnston, J. C. Bonde, J. J. White, A. Graham, Jr., Wm. Terry, Wm. A. Anderson, John S. Mosby, John Echols, Thos. S. Flournoy, Robert Stiles, James K. Edmondson, and such other persons as they shall associate with them, be and they are hereby incorporated by the name and style of The Lee Memorial Association." The usual corporate powers were conferred upon them, and the officers of the corporation were to be "a president, fifteen vice-presidents, a secretary, a treasurer, and an executive committee of nineteen members." The persons named above were declared the Executive Committee, with full powers to appoint officers and fill vacancies.

The Association organized under the charter May 31, 1873. At this meeting Gen. Jos. E. Johnston was elected President of the Association to succeed Gen. John C. Breckenridge, who had died. Col. Bolivar Christian and Capt. Walter Bowie were elected members of the Executive Committee in place of Col. J. W. Massie (deceased) and of Col. John S. Mosby (unable to serve). Gen. Pendleton was elected Chairman of the Executive Committee, C. M. Figgat, Esq., Treasurer, and Capt. C. A. Davidson, Secretary. Subsequently the Rev. J. W. Jones, D. D., was made a member of the Executive Committee in place of Major Robt. Stiles.

The funds contributed up to this time were sufficient to justify the committee in ordering the completion of the figure in marble, and in July, 1873, the artist was instructed to go forward and finish his task.

On April 1, 1875, Mr. Valentine reported the work done, and the Association took steps to have the monument brought to Lexington. At this time the students of Richmond College made application for the "privilege of taking charge of the monument when it is sent up to Lexington, and bearing the expenses of its transportation." This kind and courteous proposal was cordially accepted by the Executive Committee, and the monument was brought by canal from Richmond under an escort of the students of Richmond College. The escort was composed of Messrs. J. T. E. Thornhill, W. M. Turpin, R. H. Pitt, A. M. Harris, H. C. Smith and J. W. Martin, of Virginia; S. S. Woodward, of New Jersey; R. T. Hanks, of Alabama, and C. N. Donaldson, of South Carolina. As the figure was being taken from the artist's studio to the boat landing in Richmond, on April 13, a large number of the citizens of Richmond, headed by the students of Richmond College and the First Virginia Regiment, followed in procession to honor the memory of Lee. The monument reached Lexington April 17, 1875. Mr. Thornhill, in appropriate terms, delivered it to the committee, on whose behalf ex-Gov. John Letcher responded. Addresses were also made on this occasion by Lt. Gen. Early and Col. W. Preston Johnston. The monument was temporarily stored in a room upon the grounds of Washington and Lee University, and confided, for the time, to the guardianship of the students of that institution.

When the completion of the figure had been assured, the Executive Committee turned their attention to providing a suitable mausoleum in which it might be placed. Gen. R. D. Lilly was appointed agent to collect funds for this purpose in the winter of 1874-5. Through his efforts a handsome sum was realized, and in February, 1875, a committee was appointed to invite from architects designs for a suitable mausoleum.

The chairman of this committee, Prof. J. J. White, devoted much time and labor to conferences and correspondence with eminent architects on this subject; and many suggestions were proposed to the committee. Prominent among these was a design kindly presented in December, 1875, by Mr. J. L. Smithmeyer, of Washington, which seemed to the Executive Committee to be marked by such taste and beauty that it was determined to adopt it if the estimated cost should be found not greater than the sum the Association might expect to realize from contributions within a reasonable time. It was found, however, (in August, 1876,) when the plans and estimates were fully made, that the cost of this building would be $45,000, which the committee deemed to be far in excess of their probable resources. Meantime donations had come in from various places. The ladies of Baltimore sent, in May, 1875, $1,319.82, the result of an entertainment given by them. Subsequently there came from Charleston, S. C., $1,167.11, and from New Orleans, $1,548, from Mobile, $539.65, and valuable donations from Washington, D. C., Staunton, Va., and Camden, S. C. A handsome contribution (over $500) came from Texas, where Mr. J. S. Sullivan, of Galveston, displayed great and efficient interest in the matter. The committee were also indebted to Cyrus H. McCormick, Esq., of Chicago, for $500, and to W. A. Stuart, Esq., of Saltville, Va., for $100, as well as to many other gentlemen for smaller sums. In the summer of 1876 it seemed to the Executive Committee, from their progress so far, that they might expect the contributions for a mausoleum to reach an aggregate of $10,000 or $15,000, but not more. They therefore laid aside Mr. Smithmeyer's plan and directed their committee to select one more in accordance with their means.

A year now passed, and in May, 1877, J. Crawford Neilson, Esq., a leading architect of Baltimore, offered to furnish a design for the mausoleum. Mr. Neilson's kind offer was accepted and he was invited to visit Lexington. After full conference and investigation Mr. Neilson proposed as the design for the mausoleum a rectangular apse to be placed in the rear of the chapel of the University, where General Lee was buried. His plan was approved and adopted by the Association. As described at the time, it "consists of a fire proof apse, an addition to the rear of the chapel, conforming in material and design to the chapel itself. The lower story is a crypt of massive stone masonry, and the superstructure is built of brick. The interior is encrusted with brick and Cleveland stone, of subdued tints, and is lighted from above. The whole constitutes a solemn and tender memorial of the warrior who rests in peace beneath, surrounded by the ashes of those who were dearest on earth."

The ceremonies of laying the corner-stone took place on November 29, 1878. On this occasion Prof. J. J. White made a statement of the work of the Association, and then introduced U. S. Senator R. E. Withers, who delivered an eloquent address. After this, Gen. Jos. E. Johnston, the President of the Association, assisted by the Hon. J. Randolph Tucker, proceeded to lay the corner-stone. This is on the northeast corner of the building, about ten feet above the ground.

In February, 1879, the Association lost by death Capt. C. A. Davidson, its secretary, and one of the most active and efficient members of the Executive Committee. His contributions of time and money to the Association had been very liberal, his labors in its behalf earnest and useful, and these had extended over the entire period from its organization to his death. A. T. Barclay, ensign 4th Va. Regiment, was elected to fill the vacancy thus caused in the Executive Committee, and Capt. J. C. Boude was appointed secretary.

In January, 1879, a statement of the condition of the work was prepared by Col. W. Preston Johnston, and published, and additional subscriptions were asked for to complete it. Among the generous responses was that of W. W. Corcoran, Esq., who having heretofore given $1,000 for the figure, now added $1,000 for the mausoleum. Moro Philips, Esq., of Philadelphia, donated $500, and Geo. W. Childs, Esq., of Philadelphia, W. C. Rives, Esq., and F. R. Rivers, Esq., of New York, Robt. Garrett, Esq., of Baltimore, Hon. Wm. Milnes, Hon. J. R.

Tucker, Prof. C. A. Graves, Jno. D. Sterrett, Esq., and Col. J. D. H. Ross, of Virginia, and Col. R. G. Cole, of Georgia, each $100. Several of the resident members of the Executive Committee had each contributed previously $100. A considerable amount was added by means of musical entertainments kindly given by the ladies of Lexington, under the direction of Mrs. Judge McLaughlin. Additions were also made to the funds through some entertainments given at different places by Profs. Cromwell and Wheeler.

The building of the mausoleum was carried forward during 1879 and 1880, but the funds of the Association became exhausted before the iron roof and the interior were complete.

In the spring of 1882 the Association made a proposition to the trustees of Washington and Lee University, on the grounds of which the mausoleum stands, offering to transfer the building and monument to them in perpetual trust upon their completing the mausoleum. From a statement embodied in this proposition, it appeared that the Association had collected and expended between $23,000 and $24,000 upon the figure and mausoleum, and that $5,000 were needed in addition to complete the entire work. This proposal was accepted by the trustees of the University on April 11, 1882, and the necessary appropriation made. The agreement provided: "That upon the completion of the mausoleum and its inauguration under the auspices of this Association the title to, and the care and custody of, both the mausoleum and the marble statue of General Lee shall be vested in the corporation of Washington and Lee University, upon the sacred trust that the mausoleum shall be preserved as a perpetual place of sepulture for the remains of Gen. R. E. Lee, and of Mrs. Lee, and of such other members of their family as it may be the pleasure of the family to have interred there, and that the building and statue shall receive from the authorities of the University such care and attention from time to time as shall be needful for their preservation; and upon the further trust that neither the mausoleum, nor the ground upon which it is erected, nor the statue and appurtenances of the mausoleum, shall ever be in any way, or to any extent, liable for any claim against, or debt of said University, or be charged with any mortgage, deed of trust, or other encumbrance."

The Executive Committee of the Lee Memorial Association thus finally secured the completion of their labor of love. For twelve years it had been in progress. Many doubts had at times discouraged, many difficulties had delayed them, but the satisfaction now derived from a certainty of success more than compensated for all these. Measures were taken for the completion of the building and the placing of the figure, and the 28th of June, 1883, was selected as the day for unveiling it to the public.

In accordance with a long cherished design, the Hon. Jefferson Davis, the former President of the Confederate States, was invited to deliver on that day an address upon General Lee's military career. The Hon. Jno. W. Daniel, of Virginia, was invited to deliver, on the same occasion, an address on General Lee's life and character as a citizen and civilian. Ex-President Davis, though deeply interested in the occasion and anxious to do all in his power to honor the memory of Lee, was finally forced by advancing years and precarious health to decline, and to Major Daniel was committed the whole of the splendid theme.

The mausoleum was complete, the monument had been put in place, and the committee looked forward with pleasure to the day which should witness the end of their work and the unveiling of the figure to the public. Ere this day arrived, however, their venerable chairman, Gen. W. N. Pendleton, was summoned to join his great commander. His death on January 15, 1883, closed a long and distinguished career of honorable service to his generation, both in war and peace. He acted as Chairman of the Executive Committee of this Association, from its organization, for more than twelve years, and was most zealous and active in promoting its objects. The various relations in which he had stood to General Lee, intensified his interest in the purposes of the Association, and no one worked more earnestly for their attainment.

Judge Wm. McLaughlin was elected chairman to fill the place left vacant by the death of General Pendleton.

The final arrangements having been completed under the supervision of the architect, Mr. Neilson, and the artist, Mr. Valentine, the monument was formally transferred to the Association by Mr. Valentine on May 7, 1883, and was accepted on their behalf by the Hon. W. A. Anderson, who in fitting terms gave expression to the appreciation and admiration felt by all present as they looked upon the beautiful creation of the genius of Valentine and realized the perfection of the arrangements made by the skill and taste of Mr. Neilson for its preservation and display.

The dimensions of the mausoleum on the ground plan are 31x36 feet. The lower story, which is constructed of coraline limestone to correspond with the basement of the chapel, is a crypt containing cells or receptacles for twenty-eight bodies. Three of these contain the ashes of Gen. R. E. Lee, Mrs. Mary Custis Lee, and Miss Agnes Lee. Adjoining the crypt, but underneath the chapel, is the room used as an office by General Lee during the later years of his presidency of Washington College, which is preserved as he left it on the day he was taken ill.

The chamber containing the monument is directly over the crypt and is of brick like the corresponding part of the chapel. "The floor of the chamber is tessellated with white-veined marble and encaustic tiles. The walls consist of panels of grayish Indiana marble enframed in dark Baltimore pressed brick, and surmounted by semicircular compartments which can be used for *basso-rilievo* medallions. In one of these compartments, immediately facing the chapel, is inscribed the name of General Lee, together with the dates of his birth and death. Immediately around the base of the sarcophagus is a border of dark tiling. The tessellated floor is on the level of the platform of the chapel, which is raised three feet above the floor of the audience chamber.

"The figure and couch, which are of statuary marble, are

mounted on a sarcophagus simple almost to severity in its order, and which rests on a granite base course. The sides of the sarcophagus are composed of two marble panels each, the space between the panels bearing, in *basso-rilievo*, on the one side the Lee coat of arms, and on the other the arms of Virginia. The head and foot consist of one panel each, the former being ornamented by a simple cross, the latter bearing the legend :

ROBERT EDWARD LEE.
BORN
January 19, 1807;
DIED
October 12, 1870.

" The figure is over life size, and rests upon a heavily draped couch in an attitude of easy repose, the head being elevated to a natural position, with the face turned slightly to the right. The feet are lightly crossed. The right forearm lies across the breast--the hand holding by simple weight the blanket which covers the lower part of the body—while the left arm is fully extended along the couch, this hand holding the hilt of a sword." The contour of the limbs is easily discerned through the covering which falls over the lower part of the body.

An anti-chamber connects the monument chamber with the chapel and is separated from the former by iron doors. A large arched opening, heavily curtained, leads from the chapel into this anti-chamber. The monument is so placed and the light, which falls from the roof, so arranged, that when the curtains are drawn and the iron doors open, the figure can be seen from nearly every part of the floor and galleries of the chapel.

The 28th of June, the day for the public opening of the mausoleum, was the day after the Commencement of Washington and Lee University, the exercises of which had already drawn many persons to Lexington. In addition to these a much larger concourse of ex-Confederate soldiers gathered from every quarter on the day itself. All old Confederates and all admirers of General Lee were invited to attend, and special cards were sent to all former cabinet officers of the Confederate

States, the general officers of the Confederate army, the principal officers of the Confederate navy, the members of General Lee's staff, the Governors of the Southern States, the executive and judicial officers of Virginia, and the representatives in Congress and the Senators from Virginia. No effort was spared by the people of Lexington and Rockbridge county to honor the day. Business was suspended, and the people devoted themselves to the exercises of the day, and to entertaining the crowds that came from a distance. Special trains on the Richmond & Alleghany and the Shenandoah Valley railroads brought numbers from every point within reach. A large number of the survivors of the Stonewall Brigade, as well as of other commands of the Army of Northern Virginia, were present. Prominent among those on the ground were the Maryland Line, consisting of the survivors of the soldiers and sailors of that State, who had served in the Confederate army and navy. Besides residents of the town and county, there were present among the distinguished persons from a distance, Gen. Wade Hampton, Gen. J. A. Early, Gen. Fitz. Lee, Gen. W. H. F. Lee, Gen. Wm. Terry, Gen. Geo. H. Steuart, Gen. M. D. Corse, Gen. R. D. Lilly, Col. Wm. Norris, Chief of the Confederate Signal Bureau, Col. H. E. Peyton and Col. T. M. R. Talcott, of General Lee's Staff, Col. W. H. Palmer, of Gen. A. P. Hill's Staff, Capt. R. E. Lee, Capt. J. H. H. Figgat, Maj. E. L. Rogers, Judge H. W. Bruce, Judge J. H. Fulton, Hon. C. R. Breckinridge of Arkansas, Father Ryan, Rev. Dr. Alexander, Leigh Robinson, Esq., John J. Williams, Esq., C. W. Button, Esq., and D. Gardner Tyler, Esq. Mrs. Gen. Stonewall Jackson, Mrs. Gen. J. E. B. Stewart, Mrs. Gen. Geo. E. Pickett and Mrs. Carlisle (formerly Mrs. Gen. Geo. B. Anderson), were also present. The venerable philanthropist, W. W. Corcoran, Esq., of Washington, and the venerable ex-Gov. Wm. Smith, of Virginia, honored the occasion by their presence.

In the morning a procession was formed under General Hampton as chief marshall, which visited the grave of Stonewall Jackson in the Lexington Cemetery. Here were seen many touching evidences of the devotion of his people to this great soldier. The soldiers of the Maryland Line, under Gen. G. H. Steuart, who had shared in many of Jackson's campaigns, brought a handsome bronze tablet inscribed with the arms of Maryland, which they placed at the head of his grave. The grave itself was covered with flowers and immortelles placed there by a number of ladies under the direction of Miss Edmonia Waddell. The railing around it was similarly decorated, and at each corner was a shield surrounded by an evergreen wreath, and containing a motto furnished by Mrs. Margaret J. Preston. These mottoes were:

1. "Faith that could not fail nor yield,
    Was the legend of his shield."
        "Port Republic."

2. "From the land for which he bled,
    Honor to the warrior dead."
        "Manassas."

3. "From the field of death and fame,
    Borne upon his shield he came."
        "Chancellorsville."

4. "In the Valley let me lie,
    Underneath God's open sky."
        "Lexington."

More precious still was the silent tear which forced its way to the eye of many an old soldier as the green grave brought the scenes of twenty years ago before his sight. Among the beautiful incidents of the day was the following: The daughter of Ex-President Davis, Miss Winnie Davis, had sent to General Early two floral designs composed entirely of immortelles and made to represent the Confederate battle flag. They were exquisite in design and finish. One was intended for the grave of Lee and the other for that of Jackson. General Early selected Miss Carrie W. Daniel, the little ten-year-old daughter of the orator of the day, to place the tribute upon Jackson's grave. The tomb of Lee had been beautifully decorated with evergreens and flowers by a committee of the ladies of Lexington under the direction of Mrs. Gen. Edwin G. Lee. Amid these decorations was placed the Confederate battle flag in immortelles. After the ceremonies of the day were over, many a bronzed and gray-headed soldier might have been seen culling some of these beautiful immortelles from the graves of Lee and Jackson to commit as a sacred memento to the keeping of his children.

The procession returned from the cemetery to the grounds of Washington and Lee University, where in front of the chapel a stand and seats had been placed for the accommodation of the audience and speaker. The day was a propitious one. It was rainless, cool and bright. By 11 o'clock a mass of from 8,000 to 10,000 people filled the grounds. As many of them as could get within sound of the orator's voice gathered about the stand, and listened with absorbed attention. In the absence of Gen. Jos. E. Johnston, who was detained at home by serious illness, Lt.-General Early, the first Vice-President of the Association, presided. After prayer by the Rev. R. J. McBryde, Gen. Early introduced Maj. Daniel, who for three hours held his audience by the spell of his eloquence, moving it now to applause, and now to tears. At the close of the speech, Gen. Early called upon Father Ryan to recite his poem, "The Sword of Lee." As the poet's voice gradually rose and spread over the throng the intense emotion with which his form and his words were filled spread too, and fairly thrilled the great audience.

The moment for the unveiling of the figure was then announced by a salute fired by the survivors of the "Rockbridge Artillery," who used for the purpose two guns which had constituted a part of their armament at the first battle of Manassas. These guns were part of the cadet battery used by Stonewall Jackson when a professor at the Virginia Military Institute, and are now again in the keeping of that Institution. Some fifty of the former members of this famous artillery company had assembled for the occasion, and under Col. Wm. T. Poague, who had long been their captain, for a few moments resumed their former organization and duties. What memories of the past, what deeds of daring, and what days of toil, what moving incidents of camp and field did the sound of those guns recall as those old soldiers looked into the faces or grasped the hands they had not seen or felt for eighteen years!

As the guns opened fire the chapel and mausoleum were thrown open, the figure was unveiled by Miss Julia Jackson, (daughter of Stonewall Jackson,) and the vast throng began to move through the building to view it. For many hours the current continued its steady flow, and indeed only ceased at nightfall. Meantime the hospitable town and county was entertaining the crowd of strangers. The houses of citizens of the town were everywhere thrown open, and handsome entertainments were provided at many of them. In addition to this, a lunch, provided by the citizens of the county and town, was served on the University grounds to several thousand people.

The evening fell upon a day forever marked in the annals of Lexington. It was felt by all that Valentine's chisel had created a worthy memorial of Lee, and that Daniel, in words not less fitting had committed it to the keeping of the future.

With this day closed the active labors of the Lee Memorial Association. It only remained for them to complete the transfer of the mausoleum and monument to the perpetual care of Washington and Lee University, and to return thanks to the generous friends, who had by their contributions, rendered possible a noble work. They placed on record, in fitting terms, their high appreciation of the valuable services (services rendered as a labor of love) of their treasurer, C. M. Figgat, Esq.; of the skill and taste of J. Crawford Neilson, Esq., who placed his architectural experience gratuitously at the service of the Association in "designing and superintending the construction of the mausoleum"; of the splendid success of the artist's work, and of the oration of Major Daniel, "which can receive no higher, no juster commendation, than that it is worthy of its great subject."

A great name is passing into history. As the smoke of conflict and passion passes away the world is beginning to recognize the outlines of a character in which capacity of the first rank was harmoniously united with virtue of the highest order; a character equally grand in victory and defeat. The Lee Memorial Association have not looked upon their work as needful to preserve the fame or extend the influence of Lee, but have deemed it both a duty and a privilege to testify to coming generations the genuine affection, admiration and homage with which his countrymen and contemporaries regard the man, who seems to them the foremost of his time in those great qualities which best deserve the respect and veneration of mankind.

PROGRAMME OF CEREMONIES

AT THE

Inauguration of the Lee Mausoleum,

LEXINGTON, VIRGINIA. JUNE 28, 1883.

The following gentlemen were requested to act as Marshals and assistant Marshals, and to aid in the orderly conduct of the ceremonies of the day; and all persons were requested to respect their authority as such:

Chief Marshal—Lieutenant-General Wade Hampton.

Marshals—Gen. R. D. Lilly, Col. W. T. Poague, Col. John A. Gibson, Col. J. D. H. Ross, Maj. Charles F. Jordan, Maj. S. W. Paxton, Mr. John T. Dunlop, Mr. W. F. Johnston, Mr. Wm. M. Dunlap, Mr. Harry E. Moore, Mr. W. B. F. Leech, Mr. S. H. Letcher, Mr. J. E. McCauley, Capt. J. H. H. Figgat, Capt. T. C. Morton, Capt. Jas. A. Strain, Capt. J. G. Updike, Dr. Z. J. Walker, Capt. William Wade, Capt. J. P. Moore, Lieut. J. H. B. Jones, Mr. R. T. McLeod, Capt. W. F. Pierson, Mr. W. B. Poindexter.

Chief of Assistant Marshals—Mr. E. C. Day, of Kentucky.

Assistant Marshals—Mr. J. M. Becker, Pennsylvania; Mr. R. Godson, Kentucky; Mr. L. L. Campbell, Virginia, Mr. H. D. Flood, Virginia; Mr. J. T. Bugg, Louisiana; Mr. G. O'Bierne, West Virginia; Mr. H. McCrum, Virginia.

ORDER OF EXERCISES.

9:30 A. M. to 10:30 A. M.—Decoration of the Tomb of Lee and Grave of Jackson.

10:30 A. M.—Music on the Grounds of Washington and Lee University by the Virginia Military Institute band and visiting bands.

11 A. M.—Prayer by the Rev. R. J. McBryde, Rector of Grace Memorial Church.

MUSIC.

11:15 A. M. —Oration by Maj. John W. Daniel.

MUSIC.

2 P. M.—Figure of Lee unveiled, monumental chamber thrown open, and procession around the Figure.

3 P. M.—Collation provided by the citizens of Rockbridge and Lexington for Confederate veterans and military companies.

Seats will be set apart and reserved in front of the stand for military companies, societies, and organized bodies of veterans, of whose coming the Committee may have due notice.

The platform to the right of the stand will be set apart for representatives of the press. The other two small platforms are for the musicians of the V. M. I. band and visiting bands.

The seats upon the main stand will be reserved for:

I. Generals of the Confederate States Army and officers of the Confederate States Navy.
II. Officers of the general Government of the Confederate States.
III. The Governor of Virginia and members of the present State Government.
IV. Governors of any of the States of the Union, members of the Senate or House of Representatives of the United States.
V. Members of the Board of Trustees and Faculty of Washington and Lee University.
VI. Members of the Board of Visitors and Faculty of the Virginia Military Institute.
VII. Specially invited guests.
VIII. Members of the Lee Memorial Association.

By order of the Executive Committee,

WILLIAM McLAUGHLIN,
Chairman.
WILLIAM A. ANDERSON,
Chairman of Committee of Arrangements.
JOHN C. BOUDE,
Sec'y Ex. Com. Lee Memorial Association.

When the procession had returned from Jackson's grave to the grounds of Washington and Lee University, and those forming it had taken the seats assigned them, the exercises were opened by the Rev. R. J. McBryde, rector of Grace Memorial Church, Lexington, Va., who offered the following prayer:

Almighty and Everlasting God—the King of Kings and Lord of Lords!—our help in ages past, our hope for years to come—to Thee glory belongeth. Thou only art worthy to be praised.

For Thou art from everlasting to everlasting, Thou art gracious and full of compassion; Thou art good to all, and Thy tender mercies are over all Thy works.

We praise Thee, O God; we acknowledge Thee to be the Lord. In Thee we live and move, and have our being.

We would render unto Thee most humble and hearty thanks for the goodly heritage Thou hast given us in this land of civil and religious freedom, for the peace and prosperity within our borders, and for all the innumerable manifestations of Thy goodness towards us.

We would also recognize that it is our duty and privilege to begin, continue, and end all our works in Thee. And therefore this day, and upon this occasion, we would realize that "promotion cometh neither from the East nor from the West nor from the South. God is the judge; He putteth down one and setteth up another." Then praise to Thee alone, thou Great Creator, for the leader and commander of this people, whose memory we seek to preserve and whose name we honor to day! To Thee be all the glory for what he was and is to us. O, God, Thou wast his God; his soul followed hard after Thee; Thy right hand upheld him. He was not ashamed to confess the faith of Christ crucified and manfully to fight under His banner against sin, the world, and the devil, and to be Christ's faithful soldier and servant. And we pray Thee that the influence of his life and the power of his example may never die out in the land. May a double portion of his spirit fall on his people, whom he loved, for whom he made such sacrifices, and for whom he labored with unwearied fidelity.

May they reverence Thy name; may they retain Thee in their thoughts; may they ever live in obedience to Thy laws as did Thine honored servant: may they follow him as he followed Christ: may they love that Word which he believed, and uphold the faith which he confessed; may the well-being of our people enlist our abilities as it did his; may we, like him, seek to make the world the better for our living in it. As he was "subject to every ordinance of man for the Lord's sake," so make us to be more and more a law-abiding people, in obedience to Thy will. Give us a like patience under afflictions, and a like cheerful resignation to Thy blessed will, and by well-doing " may we put to silence the ignorance of foolish men."

Regard with Thy favor and visit with Thy blessing this institution of which he was the honored head, and secure to it the patronage needful to the carrying of its designs into good effect. And finally, when we shall have served Thee in our generation, may we, like him, be gathered unto our fathers, having the testimony of a good conscience, in the communion of the catholic church, in the confidence of a certain faith, in the comfort of a reasonable, religious, and holy hope, in favor with Thee our God, and in perfect charity with the world. All of which we ask through Jesus Christ our Lord. Amen.

GENERAL EARLY then arose and spoke as follows:

Friends, Comrades and Fellow-Citizens, Ladies and Gentlemen:

The sickness of Gen. Joseph E. Johnston, the distinguished President of the Lee Memorial Association, which prevents his attendance here, has devolved on me, as First Vice-President, the unexpected duty of presiding on this occasion; and I am sure no one can regret the cause of this change in the programme more than I do.

The great commander of the Army of Northern Virginia died on the 12th of October, 1870, and as soon as his remains were consigned to the tomb, a meeting of the citizens of Lexington was held, and steps taken for the formation of an Association to erect a monument to his memory. More effectually to carry out that purpose, an act of incorporation was obtained from the Legislature of Virginia on the 14th of January, 1871, by which certain gentlemen, most of whom were residents of Lexington, and such other persons as they should associate with themselves, were incorporated by the name and style of "The Lee Memorial Association." Subsequently the Association was further organized by the appointment of Gen. John C. Breckinridge, of Kentucky, who had been the last Secretary of War of the Confederate States, as President, and of fifteen Vice-Presidents, as also a Treasurer,—the nineteen persons named in the act of incorporation, by the terms of the act itself, constituting the Executive Committee. The chairman of that Committee was Gen. Wm. N. Pendleton, the distinguished Chief of Artillery of the Army of Northern Virginia, and the Secretary was Captain Charles A. Davidson, a gallant officer of the First Virginia Battalion.

The act of incorporation does not specify the place at which the proposed monument should be erected, nor the nature of it; but, after the passage of the act changing the name of Washington College to that of Washington and Lee University, it was determined by the Executive Committee, with the sanction of the authorities of the University, that the monument should consist of a Mausoleum, attached to the University Chapel, which latter had been constructed under the supervision of General Lee himself, where his remains should be deposited in a vault, to be surmounted by a recumbent figure in marble, representing our great chieftain at rest—it being part of the plan to provide vaults also in the same Mausoleum for the immediate members of his family, especially the estimable and noble lady who had been his partner in life.

The resident members of the Executive Committee proceeded to carry out this scheme with great energy and perseverance, in which the Chairman and Secretary were especially conspicuous. A distinguished Virginia artist was selected to execute in marble the recumbent figure, and years ago he completed his work in a manner that links his name forever with that of Lee.

Upon the death of General Breckinridge, General Joseph E. Johnston, the senior surviving officer of the Confederate Army, and the predecessor of General Lee in command of that army, which, under the lead of the latter, became so renowned as the Army of Northern Virginia, was made the President.

On the 29th of November, 1878, the corner-stone of the Mausoleum was laid, under the superintendence of a distinguished architect of Baltimore, who was charged with its construction. The requisite funds have been raised by great exertion, a large part having been contributed in small sums. The noble work has now been completed, and we are assembled here to perform the crowning act, in unveiling the recumbent figure of one of the grandest and noblest heroes, soldiers, and patriots, who have figured in all the history of the world. In doing this, we are not conferring honor on the memory of General Robert E. Lee—we are merely demonstrating to the world that we were worthy to have been the followers and compatriots of such a man. Unfortunately, neither the gallant soldier and Christian gentleman, Gen. Pendleton, Chairman of the Executive Committee, nor the gallant Davidson, the efficient Secretary of that Committee, have survived to witness the completion of the work, to the success of which they contributed so largely.

It is deeply to be regretted that President Davis, who was expected to deliver an address on this occasion, has been prevented by circumstances from being present, but his lovely and accomplished young daughter, whose pride it is to have been born on the soil of Virginia, has sent from his Southern home two Confederate flags made of immortelles, and two bay wreaths, one of each to be placed on the tombs of Generals Lee and Jackson, respectively, as tokens of her admiration for their great characters, and of the sympathy of her family with us. There is also another whose absence is to be deeply regretted, though he is nearly within reach of my voice—I mean that war Governor of Virginia, who conferred upon Generals Lee and Jackson the commissions which brought them into the service of their native State, in defence of right, justice, liberty, and independence; and who sustained them throughout, whether they were in the State or Confederate service, with such unswerving fidelity and unselfish devotion—you must know that I can mean no other than John Letcher, with whom we all so heartily sympathize in the bodily affliction which alone prevents him from being with us.

And now permit me to introduce to you, as the orator of the occasion, Major John W. Daniel, who needs no words of commendation from me, but will speak for himself.

Major Daniel was received with rounds of applause. When this had subsided he delivered the following oration :

ADDRESS OF JOHN W. DANIEL, LL. D.

Mr. President, My Comrades and Countrymen:

There was no happier or lovelier home than that of Colonel Robert Edward Lee, in the spring of 1861, when for the first time its threshold was darkened with the omens of civil war.

Crowning the green slopes of the Virginia Hills that overlook the Potomac, and embowered in stately trees, stood the venerable mansion of Arlington, facing a prospect of varied and imposing beauty. Its broad porch, and wide-spread wings, held out open arms, as it were, to welcome the coming guest. Its simple Doric columns graced domestic comfort with a classic air. Its halls and chambers were adorned with the portraits of patriots and heroes, and with illustrations and relics of the great revolution, and of the Father of his country And within and without, history and tradition seemed to breathe their legends upon a canvass as soft as a dream of peace.

The noble river, which in its history, as well as in its name, carries us back to the days when the red man trod its banks, sweeps in full and even flow along the forefront of the landscape; while beyond its waters stretch the splendid avenues and rise the gleaming spires of Washington; and over all, the great white dome of the National Capital looms up against the eastern sky, like a glory in the air.

Southward and westward, toward the blue rim of the Alleghanies, roll away the pine and oak clad hills, and the fields of the "Old Dominion," dotted here and there with the homes of a people of simple tastes and upright minds, renowned for their devotion to their native land, and for their fierce love of liberty; a people who had drunk into their souls with their mother's milk, that Man is of right, and ought to be, free.

On the one hand there was impressed upon the most casual eye that contemplated the pleasing prospect, the munificence and grandeur of American progress, the arts of industry and commerce, and the symbols of power. On the other hand, Nature seemed to woo the heart back to her sacred haunts, with vistas of sparkling waters, and verdant pastures, and many a wildwood scene; and to penetrate its deepest recesses with the halcyon charm that ever lingers about the thought of *Home.*

THE HOST OF ARLINGTON.

The head of the house established here was a man whom Nature had richly endowed with graces of person, and high qualities of head and heart. Fame had already bound his brow with her laurel, and Fortune had poured into his lap her golden horn. Himself a soldier, and Colonel[*] in the army of the United States, the son of the renowned "Light Horse Harry Lee," who was the devoted friend and compatriot of Washington in the revolutionary struggle, and whose memorable eulogy upon his august Chief has become his epitaph;—descended indeed from a long line of illustrious progenitors, whose names are written on the brightest scrolls of English and American history, from the conquest of the Norman at Hastings, to the triumph of the Continentals at Yorktown,—he had already established his own martial fame at Vera Cruz, Cerro Gordo, Contreras, Cherubusco, Molino del Rey, Chepultepec and Mexico, and had proved how little he depended upon any merit but his own. Such was his early distinction, that

---

Appointed Colonel March 16th, 1861.

when but a Captain, the Cuban Junta had offered to make him the leader of their revolutionary movement for the independence of Cuba;—a position which as an American officer, he felt it his duty to decline. And so deep was the impression made of his genius and his valor, that General Scott, Commander-in-Chief of the army in which he served, had declared that he "was the best soldier he ever saw in the field," "the greatest military genius in America," that "if opportunity offered, he would show himself the foremost Captain of his times," and that "if a great battle were to be fought for the liberty or slavery of the country, his judgment was that the commander should be Robert Lee."

Wedded to her who had been the playmate of his boyhood, and who was worthy in every relation to be the companion of his bosom, sons and daughters had risen up to call them blessed, and there, decorated with his country's honors and surrounded by "love, obedience, and troops of friends," the host of Arlington seemed to have filled the measure of generous desire with whatever of fame or happiness fortune can add to virtue. And had the pilgrim started in quest of some happier spot than the Vale of Rasselas, well might he have paused by this threshold and doffed his "sandal shoon."

THE ANTECEDENTS OF COLONEL LEE.

So situated was Colonel Lee in the spring of 1861, upon the verge of the momentous revolution, of which he became so mighty a pillar and so glorious a chieftain. But we cannot estimate the struggle it cost him to take up arms against the Union—nor the sacrifice he made, nor the pure devotion with which he consecrated his sword to his native State—without looking beyond his physical surroundings, and following further the suggestions of his history and character, for the springs of action which prompted his course. Colonel Lee was emphatically a Union man; and Virginia, to the crisis of dissolution, was a Union State. He loved the Union with a soldier's ardent loyalty to the Government he served, and with a patriot's faith and hope in the institutions of his country. His ancestors had been among the most distinguished and revered of its founders; his own life from youth upward had been spent and his blood shed in its service, and two of his sons, following his footsteps, held commissions in the army.

He was born in the same county, and descended from the same strains of English blood from which Washington sprang, and was united in marriage with Mary Custis, the daughter of his adopted son. He had been reared in the school of simple manners and lofty thoughts which belonged to the elder generation; and with Washington as his exemplar of manhood and his ideal of wisdom, he reverenced his character and fame and work with a feeling as near akin to worship as any that man can have for aught that is human.

Unlike the statesmen of the hostile sections, who were constantly thrown into the provoking conflicts of political debate, he had been withdrawn by his military occupations from scenes calculated to irritate or chill his kindly feelings toward the people of the North; and on the contrary—in camp, and field, and social circle—he had formed many ties of friendship with its most esteemed soldiers and citizens. With the reticence becoming his military office, he had taken no part in the controversies which preceded the fatal rupture between the States —other than the good man's part, to "speak the soft answer that turns away wrath," and to plead for that forbearance and patience which alone might bring about a peaceful solution of the questions at issue.

Years of his professional life he had spent in Northern communities, and, always a close observer of men and things, he well understood the vast resources of that section, and the hardy, industrious, and resolute character of its people; and he justly weighed their strength as a military power. When men spoke of how easily the South would repel invasion he said: "You forget that we are all Americans." And when they prophesied a battle and a peace, he predicted that it would take at least four years to fight out the impending conflict. None was more conscious than he that each side undervalued and misunderstood each other. He was, moreover, deeply imbued with the philosophy of history, and the course of its evolutions, and well knew that in an upheaval of government deplorable results would follow, which were not thought of in the beginning. or, if thought of, would be disavowed, belittled and deprecated. And eminently conservative in his cast of mind and character, every bias of his judgment, as every tendency of his history, filled him with yearning and aspiration for the peace of his country and the perpetuity of the Union. Is it a wonder, then, as the storm of revolution lowered, Colonel Lee, then with his regiment, the Second Cavalry, in Texas, wrote thus to his son in January, 1861 :

"The South, in my opinion, has been aggrieved by the acts of the North as you say. I feel the aggression, and am willing to take any proper steps for redress. It is the principle I contend for, not individual or private benefit. As an American citizen, I take great pride in my country, her prosperity and institutions, and would defend any State if her rights were invaded. But I can anticipate no greater calamity for the country than a dissolution of the Union. It would be an accumulation of all evils we complain of, and I am willing to sacrifice everything but honor for its preservation. I hope, therefore, that all constitutional means will be exhausted before there is a resort to force. Secession is nothing but revolution. * * Still, a Union that can only be maintained by swords and bayonets, and in which strife and civil war are to take the place of love and kindness, has no charm for me. I shall mourn for my country and for the welfare and progress of mankind. If the Union is dissolved, and the government is disrupted, I shall return to my native State and share the miseries of my people, and, save in defence, will draw my sword on none."

WAR.

A few weeks later Colonel Lee was ordered, and came to Washington, reaching there three days before the inauguration of President Lincoln. At that time South Carolina, Mississippi. Florida, Alabama, Georgia and Louisiana, had already seceded from the Union, and the Provisional Government of the Confederate States was in operation at Montgomery.

The Virginia Convention was in session, but slow and deliberate in its course. The State which had done so much to found the Union was loth to assent to its dissolution, and still guided by the wise counsels of such men as Robert E. Scott, Robert Y. Conrad, Jubal A. Early, John B. Baldwin, Samuel McDowell Moore, and A. H. H. Stuart, she persisted in efforts to avert the calamity of war. Events followed swiftly. The Peace Conference had failed. Overtures for the peaceful evacuation of Fort Sumpter had likewise failed. On the 13th of April, under bombardment, the Federal Commander, Major Anderson, with its garrison, surrendered. On April 15th President Lincoln issued his proclamation for 75,000 men to make war against the seceded States, which he styled : " Combinations too powerful to be suppressed by the ordinary course of judicial proceedings." This proclamation determined Virginia's course. War had come. Her mediation had been in vain. She was too noble to be neutral.

Of the arts of duplicity she knew nothing save to despise. She must now level her guns against the breasts of her Southern brethren, or make her own breast their shield. On April 17th Virginia answered Mr. Lincoln's proclamation with the Ordinance of Secession, and like Pallas-Athene, " the front fighter" stepped with intrepid brow to where, in conflict, history has ever found her—to the front of war.

"UNDER WHICH FLAG?"

Where now is Robert Lee? On the border line, between two hostile empires, girding their loins for as stern a fight as ever tested warriors' steel, he beholds each beckoning to him to lead its people to battle. On the one hand, Virginia, now in the fore-front of a scarcely organized revolution, summons him to share her lot in the perilous adventure. The young Confederacy is without an army. There is no navy. There is no currency. There are few teeming work-shops and arsenals. There is little but a meagre and widely scattered population, for the most part men of the field, the prairie, the forest and the mountain, ready to stand the hazard of an audacious endeavor, to meet aggression with whatever weapons freemen can lay their hands on, and to carry high the banners of the free, whatever may betide.

Did he fail? Ah, did he fail? His beloved State would be trampled in the mire of the ways; the Confederacy would be blotted from the family of nations,—home and country would survive only in memory and in name; his people would be captives, their very slaves their masters; and he,—if of himself he thought at all,—he, mayhap, might have seen in the dim perspective, the shadow of the dungeon or the scaffold.

On the other hand stands the foremost and most powerful Republic of the earth, rich in all that handiwork can fashion or that gold can buy. It is thickly populated. Its regular army, and its myriad volunteers, rush to do its bidding. Its navy rides the Western seas in undisputed sway. Its treasury teems with the sinews of war, and its arsenals with weapons. And the world is open to lend its cheer and aid and comfort. Its capital lies in sight of his chamber window, and its guns bear on the portals of his home. A messenger comes from its President and from General Scott, Commander-in-Chief of its army, to tender him supreme command of its forces. Did he accept it, and did he succeed, the conqueror's crown awaits him, and win or lose, he will remain the foremost man of a great established nation, with all honor and glory that riches and office and power and public applause can supply.

Since the Son of Man stood upon the Mount, and saw "all the kingdoms of the earth and the glory thereof" stretched before him, and turned away from them to the agony and bloody sweat of Gethsemane, and to the Cross of Calvary beyond, no follower of the meek and lowly Saviour can have undergone more trying ordeal, or met it with higher spirit of heroic sacrifice.

There was naught on earth that could swerve Robert E. Lee from the path where, to his clear comprehension, honor and duty lay. To the statesman, Mr. Francis Preston Blair, who brought him the tender of supreme command, he answered:

"Mr. Blair, I look upon secession as anarchy. If I owned

the four millions of slaves in the South, I would sacrifice them all to the Union. But how can I draw my sword against Virginia?"

Draw his sword against Virginia? Perish the thought! Over all the voices that called him he heard the still small voice that ever whispers to the soul of the spot that gave it birth, and of her who gave it suck; and over every ambitious dream, there rose the face of the angel that guards the door of home.

On the 20th of April, as soon as the news of Virginia's secession reached him, he resigned his commission in the army of the United States, and thus wrote to his sister who remained with her husband on the Union side:

"With all my devotion to the Union, and the feeling of loyalty and duty of an American citizen, I have not been able to make up my mind to raise my hands against my relatives, my children, my home. I have, therefore, resigned my commission in the army, and save in the defence of my native State (with the sincere hope that my poor services may never be needed) I hope I may never be called upon to draw my sword."

LEE DEVOTES HIS SWORD TO HIS NATIVE STATE.

Bidding an affectionate adieu to his old friend and commander, General Scott, who mourned his loss, but nobly expressed his confidence in his motives, he repaired to Richmond. Governor John Letcher immediately appointed him to the command-in-chief of the Virginia forces, and the Convention unanimously confirmed the nomination. Memorable and impressive was the scene when he came into the presence of that body on April 23d. Its venerable President, John Janney, with brief, sententious eloquence, addressed him, and concluded saying:

"Sir, we have by this unanimous vote expressed our convictions that you are at this day, among the living citizens of Virginia, 'first in war.' We pray to God most fervently that you may so conduct the operations committed to your charge, that it may be said of you that you are 'first in peace,' and when that time comes, you will have earned the still prouder distinction of being 'first in the hearts of your countrymen.'

"Yesterday your mother, Virginia, placed her sword in your hand upon the implied condition that we know you will keep in letter and in spirit: that you will draw it only in defence, and that you will fall with it in your hand rather than the object for which it was placed there should fail."

General Lee thus answered:

"*Mr. President and Gentlemen of the Convention:*

"Profoundly impressed with the solemnity of the occasion, for which I must say I was not prepared, I accept the position assigned me by your partiality. I would have preferred had your choice fallen upon an abler man. Trusting in Almighty God, an approving conscience, and the aid of my fellow-citizens, I devote myself to the service of my native State, in whose behalf alone will I ever again draw my sword."

Thus came Robert E. Lee to the State of his birth and to the people of his blood in their hour of need! Thus, with as chaste a heart as ever plighted its faith until death, for better or for worse, he came to do, to suffer, and to die for us, who to-day are gathered in awful reverence, and in sorrow unspeakable, to weep our blessings upon his tomb.

LEE'S VINDICATION—A PEOPLE IS ITS OWN JUDGE.

I pause not here to defend the course of General Lee, as that defence may be drawn from the Constitution of a Republic which was born in the sublime protest of its people against bayonet rule, and founded on the bed-rock principle of free government, that all free governments "must derive their just powers from the consent of the governed." I pause not to trace the history or define the grounds of that theory of constitutional construction which maintained the right of secession from the Union as an element of sovereign statehood—a theory which has found ablest and noblest advocacy in every section of the country. The tribunal is not yet formed that would hearken to such defence, nor is this the time or place to utter it. And to my mind there is for Lee and his compatriots a loftier and truer vindication than any that may be deduced from codes, constitutions, and conventional articles of government. A great revolution need never apologize for nor explain itself. There it is!—the august and thrilling rise of a whole population! And the fact that it is there is the best evidence of its right to be there. None but great inspirations underlie great actions. None but great causes can ever produce great events. A transient gust of passion may turn a crowd into a mob—a temporary impulse may swell a mob into a local insurrection; but when a whole people stand to their guns before their hearthstones, and as one man resist what they deem aggression; when for long years they endure poverty and starvation, and dare danger and death to maintain principles which they deem sacred—when they shake a continent with their heroic endeavors and fill the world with the glory of their achievements, history can make for them no higher vindication than to point to their deeds and say—"behold!"

A people is its own judge. Under God there can be no higher judge for them to seek or court or fear. In the supreme moments of national life, as in the lives of individuals, the actor must resolve and act within himself alone. The Southern States acted for themselves—the Northern States for themselves —Virginia for herself. And when the lines of battle formed, Robert Lee took his place in the line beside his people, his kindred, his children, his home. Let his defence rest on this fact alone. Nature speaks it. Nothing can strengthen it. Nothing can weaken it. The historian may compile; the casuist may dissect; the statesman may expatiate; the advocate may plead; the jurist may expound; but, after all, there can be no stronger or tenderer tie than that which binds the faithful heart to kindred and to home. And on that tie—stretching from the cradle to the grave, spanning the heavens, and riveted through eternity to the throne of God on high, and underneath in the souls of good men and true—on that tie rests, stainless and immortal, the fame of Robert Lee.

LEE'S EARLY SERVICE IN THE CONFEDERATE WAR.

And now that war was flagrant, history delights to testify how grandly General Lee bore his part. Transferred from the State service to that of the Confederacy, with the rank of General, we behold him at first in the field in the rugged mountains of Northwest Virginia, restoring the morale lost by the early reverses to our arms in that Department—holding invading columns in check with great disparity of force to meet them—bearing the censures of the impatient without a murmur, and careless of fame with duty done. Later, in the fall of 1861, we find him exercising his skill as an engineer in planning defences along the threatened coast of South Carolina; and in March, 1862, he is again in Virginia, charged by President Davis " with the conduct of military operations in the armies of the Confederacy"—in brief, and in some sort, under the President, Commander-in-Chief.

But now a year of war had rolled by; no brilliant accomplishment had yet satisfied the public expectation with which he had been welcomed as a Southern leader; and as the fame of revolutionary Captains can only be fed with victories, it is unquestionable that, at this stage of his career, the reputation of Lee, as a General, had sensibly declined.

THE FALL OF GENERAL JOSEPH E. JOHNSTON AND THE OPPORTUNITY OF LEE.

Meanwhile the Army of Northern Virginia had made a name in history under its famous commander, Joseph E. Johnston; and I cannot speak that name without bowing the homage of my heart to the illustrious soldier and noble gentleman who bears it. Under his sagacious and brilliant leadership, his forces had been suddenly witdrawn from Patterson's front near Winchester, and united with those of General Beauregard at Manassas; and there, led by these two Generals, the joint command had, on July 21st, 1861, routed the Army of the Potomac in the first pitched battle of the war; had given earnest of what the volunteers of the South could do in action, and had crowned the new-born Confederacy with the glory of splendid military achievement. Still later in the progress of events, Johnston had exhibited again his strategic skill in holding McClellan at bay on the lines of Yorktown, with a force so small that it seemed hardihood to oppose him with it—had eluded his toils by a retreat up the Peninsula, so cleanly conducted, that little was lost beyond the space vacated*—had turned and fiercely smitten his advancing columns near the old Colonial Capital of Williamsburg on May 5th, 1862, and had planted his army firmly around Richmond. Pending the siege of Yorktown, a thing had happened that probably had no parallel in history. The great body of General Johnston's army had reörganized itself under the laws of the Confederacy, while lying under the fire of the enemy's guns, the privates of each company electing by ballot the officers that were to command them. A singular exercise of suffrage was this, but there was "a free ballot and a fair count," and an exhibition worthy of

"That fierce Democracy that thundered over Greece
To Macedon and Artaxerxes' throne."

—an exhibition which would have delighted the heart of Thomas Jefferson, and which certainly put to blush the autocratic theory that armies should be mere compact masses of brute force. Still later, on May 31st, Johnston had sallied forth and stormed

*NOTE.—The Philadelphia *Times* of September 4th, 1883, contained an article from the pen of Allan B. Magruder, Esq., brother of the late distinguished Confederate officer, Major General John Bankhead Magruder, in which the writer takes exception to this statement of my address. He says that to General Magruder belongs the credit of the "strategic skill" which held McClellan at bay on the lines of Yorktown; that General Johnston never commanded on those lines; and that the Army of Northern Virginia never fired a shot in their defence.

The high character and standing of the writer, and my great respect for the memory of General Magruder, to whom I would do all honor, induce me to notice this article here. I do not deny that General Magruder did, before the arrival of General Johnston, defend the lines of Yorktown with wonderful address and boldness, and is entitled to high praise for the ability and courage displayed in so doing. Yet there can be no doubt that General Johnston did command the army defending the Yorktown lines; and that his army fired many a shot in their defence. This is attested by all the official records. That there can be no mistake about it, I am myself a witness, for I marched from Centreville to Richmond, and there took steamer for the "lines of Yorktown" with General Johnston's forces; lay with them there in the trenches for weeks, and saw and heard the firing of many a shot from cannon, rifle, and musket in their defence. And under command of General Johnston, whom I personally saw on the field, I marched with his troops on the retreat from Yorktown, and participated in the battle of Williamsburg, May 5th, 1862, with the advancing forces of McClellan.

The fact is Mr. Magruder has fallen into what is to me, a strange and unaccountable error, as he will discover on reading any history of the events referred to. I have before me McCabe's Life of Lee, and Gen. Joseph E. Johnston's work, entitled "Johnston's Narrative," and they confirm the accuracy of the statements upon which my remarks are based. The credit given General Johnston is due him; but it in no wise detracts from that likewise due General Magruder, for his anterior exploits of a like nature.　　　　　　　　　　　　J. W. D.

and taken the outer entrenchments and camps of McClellan's army at Seven Pines, capturing ten pieces of artillery, six thousand muskets, and other spoils of war, and destroying the prestige of the second "On to Richmond" movement.

But ere the day was done victory had been checked, and glory had exacted costly tribute, for Johnston himself had fallen, terribly wounded. The hero, covered with ten wounds received in Florida and Mexico, had been prostrated by another; and when June 1st dawned on the confronting armies, the Army of Northern Virginia was without the leader who held its thorough confidence, but now lay stricken well-nigh unto death. The casualty which thus deprived the army of its honored commander, and closed to him the opportunity, which, in large measure, his own great skill had created, opened the opportunity of Lee. Fortunate the State, and great the people from whom spring two such sons—fortunate the army that always had a leader worthy of it—happy he who can transmit his place to one so well qualified to fill it—and happy likewise he who had such predessor to prepare the way for victory.

GENERAL LEE IN COMMAND OF THE ARMY OF NORTHERN VIRGINIA—RICHMOND, MANASSAS, HARPER'S FERRY, SHARPSBURG, FREDERICKSBURG.

On the 3d of June, 1862, General Lee was assigned to command in person the Army of Northern Virginia; and from that day to April 9th, 1865, nearly three years, he was at its head. And on the page of history now laid open are crowded schemes of war and feats of arms as brilliant as ever thrilled the soul of heroism and genius with admiration,—a page of history that feasted glory till pity cried, "no more." Swift was Lee to plan, and swift to execute. Making a feint of reinforcing Jackson in the Valley, startling the Federal authorities with apprehensions of attack on the Potomac lines, and practically eliminating McDowell, who, with his corps, remained near Fredericksburg, he suddenly descends with Jackson on the right and rear of McClellan, and ere thirty days have passed since he assumed command. Richmond has been saved, and the fields around her made immortal; and the broken ranks of McClellan are crouching for protection under the heavy guns of the iron-clads at Harrison's Landing. Sixty days more, and the siege of Richmond has been raised,—the Confederate columns are marching Northward; Jackson in the advance, has on August 9th caught up again with his old friend Banks, at Slaughter's Mountain, and punished him terribly, and as the day closes August 30th, Manassas has the second time been the scene of a general engagement with like results as the first. John Pope, who thitherto, according to his pompous boast, had "seen only the backs of his enemies," has had his curiosity entirely satisfied with a brief glimpse of their faces; and the proud army of the Potomac is flying in hot haste to find shelter in the entrenchments of Washington. In early September the Confederates are in Maryland. In extreme exigency, McClellan is recalled to command the Army of the Potomac, but while Lee holds him in check at Boonsboro and South Mountain, a series of complicated manœuvres have invested General Miles, the officer in command at Harper's Ferry, and on September 15th Stonewall Jackson has there received surrender of his entire army of eleven thousand men, seventy-three cannon, thirteen thousand small arms, two hundred wagons, and many stores. But there is no time to rest, for McClellan presses Lee at Sharpsburg, and there, September 17th, battle is delivered. Upon its eve Jackson has arrived fresh from Harper's Ferry. McClellan's repeated assaults on Lee were everywhere repulsed. He remained on the field September 18th, and then recrossed the Potomac into Virginia.

The winter of 1862 comes, and Burnside, succeeding McClellan, assails Lee at Fredericksburg on December 13th, and is repulsed with terrible slaughter.

1863—CHANCELLORSVILLE.

With the dawn of spring in 1863, a replenished army with a fresh commander, "Fighting Joe Hooker," renews the onset by way of Chancellorsville, and finds Lee with two divisions of

Longstreet's corps absent in Southeast Virginia. But slender as are his numbers, Lee is ever aggressive; and while Hooker with "the finest army on the planet," as he styled it, is confronting Lee near Chancellorsville, and Early is holding Sedgwick at bay at Fredericksburg, Jackson, who, under Lee's directions, has stealthily marched around him, comes thundering in his rear, and alas! for "Fighting Joe," he can only illustrate his pugnacious subriquet by the consoling reflection that

> "He who fights and runs away,
> May live to fight another day,"

for Chancellorsville shines high on the list of Confederate victories, and indeed was one of the grandest victories that ever blazoned the annals of war.

THE FALL OF STONEWALL JACKSON.

But alas! too, for the victor,—on May 2d, in the culminating act of the drama, Jackson himself had fallen, and never more is the "foot cavalry" to see again along the smoking lines that calm, stern face;—never to hear again that crisp, fierce order, "Give them the bayonet!" which so often heralded the triumphant charge; never is the Southern land to be thrilled again with his familiar bulletin—"God blessed our arms with victory." At the age of 39—at a time of life when the powers of manhood are ordinarily scarce full-orbed, he has touched the zenith, and filled the world with his fame; and he who went forth two years before from this quiet town, scarce known beyond it, comes back upon the soldier's bier, renowned, revered, and mourned in every clime where the heart quickens in sympathy for surpassing valor, united with transcendent genius and honor without a stain. There he sleeps, in yon green grave, and as in life he fought, so in death he rests with Lee.

WINCHESTER AND GETTYSBURG.

But not long can the soldier pause to weep. We fire our salute over the ashes of our heroic dead; and again the bugles sound "boots and saddles," and the long roll is beating. Less than a month has passed, and again the Army of Northern

Virginia is in motion, and while Hooker is groping around to ascertain the whereabouts of his adversary, the next scene unfolds: General Early has planned and executed a flank march around Winchester, worthy of Stonewall Jackson,—the men of his division are mounting the parapets on June 14th, and capturing Milroy's guns. General Edward Johnston's division is pursuing Milroy's fugitives down the Valley pike. General Rodes has captured Martinsburg, with 100 prisoners and five cannon,—Ewell's corps is master of the Valley,—and by June 24th, the Army of Northern Virginia is in Pennsylvania, while for the third time the Army of the Potomac is glad if it can interpose to prevent the fall of Washington—and a sixth commander has come to its head—General George C. Meade.

Then follows the boldest and grandest assault of modern war—the charge upon the Federal centre entrenched on the heights of Gettysburg—a charge that well-nigh ended the war with "a clap of thunder," and was so characterized by brave design and dauntless execution that friend and foe alike burst into irrepressible praise of the great commander who directed and of the valorous men who made it. It failed. But Lee, unshaken, rallies the broken lines, and the next morning stands in steady array, flaunting his banners defiantly, and challenging renewal of the strife. "It is all my fault," he says. Not so thought his men. We saw him standing by the roadside with his bridle rein over his arm, on the second day afterwards, as the army was withdrawing. Pickett's division filed past him; every General of Brigade had fallen, and every field-officer of its regiments; a few tattered battle-flags and a few hundreds of men were all that was left of the magnificent body, 5,000 strong, who had made the famous charge. He stood with uncovered head, as if he reviewed a conquering host, and with the conqueror's look upon him. With proud step the men marched by, and as they raised their hats and cheered him there was the tenderness of devoted love, mingled with the fire of battle, in their eyes.

Returning to Virginia in martial trim and undismayed, and

followed by Meade with that slow and gingerly step which is self-explaining, we next behold our General displaying that rare self-poise and confidence which bespeaks ever a great quality—firmness of mind in war. In September, while he confronts Meade along the Rapidan, he detatches the entire corps of Longstreet, and ere Meade is aware of this weakening of his opponent's forces, Longstreet is nine hundred miles away, striking a terrible blow at Chickamauga.

The year 1863 passes by without other signticant event in the story of the Army of Northern Virginia. Meade indeed, once in November, deployed his lines along Mine Run in seeming overtures of battle, but quickly concluding that "discretion was the better part of valor," he marched back across the Rappahannock, content with his observations.

1864—WILDERNESS, SPOTSYLVANIA, COLD HARBOR, PETERSBURG, LYNCHBURG.

But as the May blossoms in 1864, we hear once more the wonted strain of spring, "tramp, tramp, tramp, the boys are marching," and Grant (who had succeeded Meade), crossing the Rappahannock with 141,000 men, plunges boldly into the Wilderness on May 4th, leading the sixth crusade for the reduction of Richmond. But scarce had he disclosed his line of march, than Lee, with 50,000 of his braves, springs upon him and hurls him back, staggering and gory, through the tangled chapparal of the Wilderness, and from the fields of Spotsylvania: and though the redoubtable Grant writes to the Government on May 12th, "I propose to fight it out on this line if it takes all summer;" when we look over the field of Cold Harbor on June 3d, we see there, stretched in swaths and piled in reeking mounds 13,000 of his men,—the killed and wounded of his last assault "in the over-land campaign." And when Grant ordered his lines to attack again the flinty front of Lee, they stood immobile,—in silent protest against the vain attempt, and in silent enlogy of their sturdy foe. One summer month had been summer time enough for Grant along that impervious line; and there at Cold Harbor practically closed

the sixth expedition aimed directly at the Confederate Capital
—McDowell, McClellan, Pope, Burnside, Hooker and now
Grant,—all being disastrously repulsed by the Army of Northern Virginia, and all but the first receiving their repulse by the army led by Lee. But Grant in some sort, veiled his reverses by immediately abandoning attack on the north side of the James, which he crossed in the middle of June,—attempting to capture Petersburg on the south side by a *coup de main*. But in this, after four days' successive assaults which ended in vain carnage, he failed again; and almost simultaneously Hunter's invasion through the Valley was intercepted and successfully repelled at Lynchburg by the swift and bold movements of Lee's greatest Lieutenant,—the ever-to-be-counted-on Jubal A. Early, who had been dispatched to meet him with a force not half his equal in numbers. And when midsummer came, Grant was glad to shelter his drooping banners behind entrenchments; Hunter was flying to the mountains of West Virginia, and detachments were hurrying from the Army of the Potomac to save Washington, which was trembling at the sound of Early's guns. In that wonderful campaign of Lee from the Wilderness to Petersburg, Grant had lost not less than 70,000 men in reaching a point which he might have gained by river approaches without the loss of one. Every man in the Army of Northern Virginia, had more than stricken down a foeman; and final demonstration had been given to the fact that in field fight, Lee could not be matched in generalship, and that the Army of Northern Virginia was invincible. This fact the hard sense of Grant recognized; and though no commander who felt himself and his men to be the equals of their adversaries in manœuvre and combat would ever come down to such conclusion, it is creditable to Grant's plain, matter-of-fact way of looking at things—that he looked at them just as they were. And so he resorted to sap and mine and pick and spade to do the work which strategy and valor had so often essayed in vain. For nine months the armies lay before the muzzles of each other's guns,—bumping, as it were, against each other,—Grant deliberately counting that he who had the

most heads could butt the longest. Thus Lee stood with less than 40,000 men covering a line of thirty miles, while Grant, with more than three times that number, over and over again at Reams's Station, at the Crater, at Hatcher's Run and other points, battered the armor from which every blow recoiled. So Lee stood with a half-fed and half-clothed soldiery, composed largely of stripling youth and failing age, beating back his three-fold foe, freshly recruited for every fresh assault, and generously provided with the richest stores and most approved arms and munitions of war.

Time forbids that I prolong the story; and this imperfect sketch is but a dim outline of that grand historic picture in which Robert Lee will ever stand as the foremost figure, challenging and enchaining the reverence and admiration of mankind,—the faint suggestion of that magnificent career which has made for him a place on the heights of history as high as warrior's sword has ever carved.

PREMONITIONS OF THE END—THE MARCH TO APPOMATTOX.

Vain was the mighty struggle, led by the peerless Lee. Genius planned, valor executed, patriotism stripped itself of every treasure, and heroism fought and bled and died,—and all in vain! When the drear winter of 1864 came at last, there came also premonotions of the end. "The very seed-corn of the Confederacy had been ground up," as President Davis said. The people sat at naked tables and slept in sheetless beds, for their apparel had been used to bind up wounds. The weeds grew in fenceless fields, for the plow-horse was pulling the cannon. The church-yard and the mansion fences were stripped of their leaden ornaments, that the musket and the rifle might not lack for bullets. The church bells, now melted into cannon, pealed forth the dire notes of war. The land was drained of its substance, and the Army of Northern Virginia was nearly exhausted for want of food and raiment. All through the bleak winter days and nights its decimated and shivering ranks still faced the dense battallions of Grant, in misery and want not less than that which stained the snows of Valley Forge; and the army seemed to live only on its innate, indomitable will, as oftentimes we see some noble mind survive when the physical powers of nature have been exhausted. Like a rock of old ocean, it had received, and broken, and hurled back into the deep in bloody foam those swiftly succeeding waves of four years of incessant battle; but now the rock itself was wearing away, and still the waves came on.

A new enemy was now approaching the sturdy devoted band. In September, 1864, Atlanta fell, and through Georgia to the sea, with fire and sword, swept the victorious columns of Sherman. In January, 1865, the head of column had been turned northward: and in February, Columbia and Charleston shared the fate that had already befallen Savannah. Yes, a new enemy was approaching the Army of Northern Virginia, and this time in the rear. The homes of the soldiers of the Army of Northern Virginia from the Southern States were now in ashes. Wives, mothers and sisters were wanderers under the winter skies, flying from the invaders who smote and spared not in their relentless march. Is it wonder that hearts that never quailed before bayonet or blade beat now with tremulous and irrepressible emotion? Is it wonder that, in the watches of the night, the sentinel in the trenches, tortured to excruciation with the thought that those dearest of earth to him were without an arm to save, felt his soul sink in anguish and his hope perish? So it was, that with hunger and nakedness as its companions, and foes in front and foes in rear, the Army of Northern Virginia seemed bound to the rock of fate.

On April 1st the left wing of Grant's massive lines swept around the right and rear of Lee. Gallantly did Pickett and his men meet and resist them at Five Forks; but that commanding strategic point was taken, and the fall of Petersburg and of Richmond alike became inevitable. On the next day, April 2d, they were evacuated. Grant was now on a shorter line projected toward Danville than Lee, and the latter commenced at once that memorable retreat towards Lynchburg, which ended at Appomattox.

THE BATTLE OF APPOMATTOX—THE LAST CHARGE.

Over that march of desperate valor disputing fate, as over the face of a hero in the throes of dissolution, I throw the blood-recking battle-flag, rent with wounds, as a veil. And I hail the heroic army and its heroic chief, as on the 9th of April morn, they stand embattled in calm and stern repose, ready to die with their harness on,—warriors every inch, without fear, without stain. Around the little hamlet of Appomattox Courthouse is gathered the remnant of the Army of Northern Virginia,—less than 8,000 men with arms in their hands,—less than 27,000 all told, counting camp followers and stragglers; and around them in massive concentric lines the army of Grant, flushed with success and expectation—more than 80,000 strong upon the field, and with each hour bringing up re-inforcements. "The environed army, with a valor all Spartan, stand ready to die, not indeed in response to civic laws denying surrender, but obedient to the lofty impulse of honor." Can they cut through? Does the dream of a saved Confederacy yet beckon them on beyond the wall of steel and fire that girdles them? Can they find fighting ground in the Carolinas with Joseph E. Johnston, who, among the first to meet the foe, proves amongst the last to leave him? Can these dauntless foeman yet cleave a path to the inner country, and renew the unequal strife?

Not till that hope is tested will they yield!

As the day dawns, a remnant of the cavalry under Fitz. Lee is forming, and Gordon's infantry, scarce two thousand strong, are touching elbows for the last charge. Once more the thrilling rebel cheer rings through the Virginia woods, and with all their wonted fierceness they fall upon Sheridan's men. Ah! yes, victory still clings to the tattered battle-flags. Yes, the troopers of our gallant Fitz. are as dauntless as when they followed the plume of Stuart, "the flower of cavaliers." Yes, the matchless infantry of "tattered uniforms and bright muskets" under Gordon, the brave, move with as swift, intrepid tread as when of old—Stonewall led the way. Soldiers of Manassas, of Richmond, Sharpsburg, Fredericksburg, Chancellorsville, Gettysburg, of the Wilderness, of Spotsylvania, of

Cold Harbor, of Petersburg—scarred and sinewy veterans of fifty fields, your glories are still about you, your manhood is triumphant still. Yes, the blue lines break before them; two cannon and many prisoners are taken, and for two miles they sweep the field towards Lynchburg—victors still!

But no, too late! too late! Behind the flying sabres and rifles of Sheridan rise the bayonets and frown the batteries of the Army of the James, under Ord—a solid phalanx stands right athwart the path of Fitz. Lee's and Gordon's men. Too late! the die is cast! The doom is sealed! There is no escape. The eagle is quarried in his eyre; the wounded lion is haunted to his lair!

And so the guns of the last charge died away in the morning air; and echo, like the sob of a mighty sea, rolled up the valley of the James, and all was still. The last fight of the Army of Northern Virginia had been fought. The end had come. The smoke vanished. The startled birds renewed their songs over the stricken field; the battle smell was drowned in the fragrance of the flowering spring. And the ragged soldier of the South, God bless him! stood there facing the dread reality, more terrible than death—stood there to grapple with and face down despair, for he had done his all, and all was lost, *save Honor!*

SURRENDER.

General Lee, dressed in his best uniform, rides to the front to meet General Grant. For several days demands for surrender had been rejected—now surrender was inevitable. And the two commanding officers meet at the McLean House to concert its terms. The first and abiding thought of Lee was the honor of his men, for he had determined to "cut his way through at all hazards, if such terms were not granted as he thought his army was entitled to demand." "General," said Lee, addressing Grant, and opening the conversation, "I deem it due to proper candor and frankness to say at the beginning of this interview that I am not willing even to discuss any terms of surrender, inconsistent with the honor of my army, which I am determined to maintain to the last." Grant gave fitting and magnanimous response, and the honorable terms demanded were agreed to. "The officers to retain their side arms, private horses and baggage," and "each officer and man to be allowed to return to his home," and, mark it, "*not to be disturbed by United States authority as long as they observe their parole, and the laws in force where they reside.*"

Thus at last was the liberty of the soldier purchased with his blood.

And so the Army of Northern Virginia, never broken in battle, passed from action into History; so it perished by the flashing of the guns, while victory hung charmed to its flag, and threw upon its tomb the immortelles of Honor.

> "The old order changeth, yielding place to new,
> And God fulfills himself in many ways."

FAREWELL.

"*Men, we have fought through the war together. I have done my best for you; my heart is too full to say more,*" was Lee's utterance to the ragged, battle-begrimmed boys in gray, who, when the dread news of surrender spread among them, gathered around him to shake his hand and testify their undying confidence and love. In his published address he said to them: "You will carry with you the satisfaction that proceeds from the consciousness of duty faithfully performed, and I earnestly pray that a merciful God will extend to you his blessing and protection. With an unceasing admiration of your constancy and devotion to your country, and a grateful remembrance of your kind and generous consideration of myself, I bid you an affectionate farewell."

As Robert Lee rode from Appomattox toward Richmond, he carried with him the heart of every man that fought under him—linked to him with hooks of steel forever. When he reached the fallen Capital of the dead Confederacy, and rode through its ashes and paling fires to his home, a body of Federal soldiers there, catching a glimpse of his noble countenance, lifted their hats and cheered; and as the great actor in the bloody drama stepped behind the scenes, and the curtain fell upon the tragic stage of the secession war, the last sounds that greeted his ears were the generous salutations of respect from those against whom he had wielded his knightly sword.

RETIREMENT, COUNSEL AND ACCEPTANCE OF THE SITUATION.

Had the paroled soldier of Appomattox carried to retirement the vexed spirit and hollow heart of a ruined gamester, nothing had remained to him but to drain the dregs of a disappointed career. But there went with him that "consciousness of duty faithfully performed," which consoles every rebuff of fortune, sweetens every sorrow, and tempers every calamity—and now it was that he proved indeed what he once expressed in language, that "Human fortitude should be equal to human adversity." Once on the Appomattox lines agony had tortured from his lips the words: "How easily I could get rid of this and be at rest. I have only to ride along the lines, and all will be over." But he quickly added: "It is our duty to live, for what will become of the women and children of the South if we are not here to protect them?" And as the thought of his country was thus uppermost and controlling in the awful hour of surrender, so it remained to the closing of his life. Ere the struggle ended he had disclosed to a confidential friend, General Pendleton, that "he never believed we could, against the gigantic combination for our subjugation, make good our independence, unless foreign powers, directly or indirectly, assisted us." But said he, "We had sacred principles to maintain and rights to defend, for which we were in duty bound to do our best, even if we perished in the endeavor." And now that this belief was verified, he declared: "I did only what my duty demanded. I could have taken no other course without dishonor. And if all were to be done over again, I should act in precisely the same manner." And when those about him mourned the great disaster, he said: "Yes, that is all very sad, and might be a cause of self-reproach, but that we are conscious that we have humbly tried to do our duty. We may, therefore, with calm satisfaction, trust in God, and leave results to Him."

Lee thoroughly understood and thoroughly accepted the situation. He realized fully that the war had settled, settled forever, the peculiar issues which had embroiled it; but he knew also that only time could dissipate its rankling passions and restore freedom; and hence it was he taught that "Silence and patience on the part of the South was the true course "— silence, because it was vain to speak when prejudice ran too high for our late enemies to listen—patience, because it was the duty of the hour to labor for recuperation and wait for reconciliation. And murmuring no vain sigh over the "might have been," which now could not be—conscious that our destinies were irrevocably bound up with those of the perpetual Union, he lifted high over the fallen standards of war the banner of the Prince of Peace, emblazoned with "Peace on Earth and Good Will toward Men."

The President and Congress of the United States made conditions of pardon and absolution. They were harsh and exacting. The mass of the people affected by them, of necessity, *had* to accept them. Therefore he would share their humiliation. Accordingly he asked amnesty. But his letter was never answered. He was indicted for treason. He appeared ready to answer the charge. But the government now revolted from an act of treachery so base, for his parole of Appomattox protected him. Thus was he reviled and harrassed, yet never word of bitterness escaped him; but, on the contrary, only counsels of forbearance, patience and diligent attention to works of restoration. Many sought new homes in foreign lands, but not so he. "All good citizens," he said, "must unite in honest efforts to obliterate the effects of war, and to restore the blessings of peace. They must not abandon their country, but go to work and build up its prosperity." "The young men especially must stay at home, bearing themselves in such a manner as to gain the esteem of every one, at the same time that they maintain their own respect." "It should be the object of all to avoid controversy, to allay passion, and give scope to every kindly feeling." "It is wisest not to keep open the sores of war, but to follow the example of those nations who have endeavored to obliterate the marks of civil strife, and to commit to oblivion the feelings it engendered."

"True patriotism sometimes requires of men to act exactly contrary at one period to that which it does at another, and the motive that impels them, the desire to do right, is precisely the same. The circumstances which govern their actions change, and their conduct must conform to the new order of things. History is full of illustrations of this. Washington himself is an example of this. At one time he fought against the French under Braddock; at another time he fought with the French at Yorktown, under the orders of the Continental Congress of America, against him. He has not been branded by the world with reproach for this, but his course has been applauded." These were some of the wise and temperate counsels with which he pointed out the duties of the hour.

JEFFERSON DAVIS.

Nor was he lacking in faithful remembrance of the President of the Confederacy, who for months and months after surrender lay sick and in prison, and who seemed to be singled out to undergo vicarious punishment for the deeds of the people. "Mr. Davis," truly said General Lee, "did nothing more than all the citizens of the Southern States, and should not be held accountable for acts performed by them, in the exercise of what had been considered by them unquestionable right." None are more conscious of this fact than those against whom Jefferson Davis directed the Confederate arms; and that he yet, nearly twenty years after strife has ceased, should be disfranchised in a land that vaunts its freedom, for so doing, is a grievance, and a grief to every honorable Southern man. He himself is honored by this significant mark of hostile memory. He cannot suffer by the ignoble act. Only they who do it are deeply ashamed. And that it is done, only shows the weakness of representatives who have not read the very title page in the book of human nature, and who, vainly conceiving that an insult to one man can be fruitful of any public good, only illustrate the saying of Madame de Staël, "that the strongest of all antipathies is that of second-rate minds for a first-rate one," and that other maxim of Edmund Burke, that "great empires and little minds go ill together." When Marc Antony, the great Triumvir of Rome, who conquered Egypt, was himself overthrown by Octavius Cæsar, he gloried dying that he " had conquered as a Roman, and was by a Roman nobly conquered." If the spirit of those brave soldiers of the Union, who, while the fields of battle were yet moist with blood, saluted Lee, had guided the conduct of the civilians to whom their valor gave the reins of State, it would have been for us Confederates who achieved great victories, and were in turn cast down, to have gloried likewise, that we in our time had conquered as Americans, and were by Americans nobly conquered. But when we recall that our honored and faithful President is disfranchised simply because he was our chief, and bravely, ably served our cause, the iron enters our souls and represses the generous emotions that well up in them. And we can only lament that shallow politicians have proven unworthy of the American name, and are not imbued with the great free spirit of a great free people. We have not a thought or fancy or desire to undo the perpetuity of the Union. For any man to pretend to think otherwise is proclamation of his falsehood, or his folly. But we intend to be free citizens of the Union, accepting no badge of inferiority or dishonor. And by the tomb of our dead hero, who was true to his chief, as to every trust, we protest to mankind against this unjust thing; an offence to our liberties and to our manhood, which are not less sacred than the grave.

And we waft to him, our late Chief Magistrate, in his Southern home, our greetings and our blessings; and as the years grow thick upon him, we pray that he may find in the unabated confidence and affection of his people, some solace for all that he has borne for them; and in the strength that cometh from on high, a staff that man cannot take from him.

MEDITATIONS OF DUTY.

While General Lee thus sustained and cheered his countrymen, the problem soon began to press, what should he do with himself? And had he been in any sense a self-seeker, the solution had been easy, for many were the overtures and proffers made to him in every form of interested solicitation, and disinterested generosity. Would he seek recreation from the trials which for years had strained every energy of mind and body, and every emotion of his heart,—the palaces of European nobility, the homes of the Old World and the New, alike, opened their doors to him as a welcome and honored guest. Would he prolong his military career? More than one potentate would have been proud to receive into his service his famous sword. Would he retrieve his fortunes and surround his declining years with luxury and wealth? He had but to yield the sanction of his name to any one of the many enterprises that commercial princes commended to his favor, with every assurance of munificent reward. And indeed, were he willing to accept, unlimited means were placed at his disposal by those who would have been proud to render him any service.

But it had been the principle of Lee's life to accept no gratuitous offer. He had declined the gift of a home tendered to him by the citizens of Richmond during the war, when Arlington had been confiscated, and the refuge of his family, the "White House," had been burned,—expressing the hope that those who offered the gift would devote the means required "to the relief of the families of our soldiers in the field, who are more deserving of assistance, and more in want of it than myself." And now when an English nobleman presented him as a retreat a splendid country seat in England, with a handsome annuity to correspond, he answered: "I am deeply grateful, but I cannot consent to desert my native State in the hour of her adversity. I must abide her fortunes and share her fate." And declining also the many positions with lucrative salaries which were urged upon his acceptance, it was his intention to locate in one of the Southside counties of Virginia, "upon a small farm where he might earn his daily bread" in cultivating the soil, and at the same time to write a history of his campaigns; "not," as he said, "to vindicate myself, and promote my own reputation, but to show the world what our poor boys with their small numbers and scant resources had succeeded in accomplishing."

But circumstances, then to him unknown, were bringing an event to pass which turned over a new and unexpected leaf in his history—an event which made a little scion of knowledge, which had been nurtured through the storms of the Colonial Revolution, a great and noble University, and which now has associated in the glorious work of education, as in glorious deeds of arms, the twin names of Washington and Lee.

LIBERTY HALL ACADEMY.

It was nearly a century after the settlement at Jamestown, that Governor Spotswood of Virginia, at the head of a troop of horse, first explored the hitherto unknown land beyond the mountains, and upon his return from the expedition, the Governor presented to each of his bold companions a golden horseshoe, inscribed with the legend: "*Sic jurat transcendere montes*," as a memorial of the event; a circumstance which caused them to be named in history. "The Knights of the Golden Horseshoe." In August, 1716, these adventurous spirits first looked down from the heights of the Blue Ridge upon the beautiful Valley of Virginia,—a virgin land indeed, tenanted only by the roving red men. Glorious must have been the thrill of joy that quickened their hearts, as the tempting vision lay spread before them, as their eyes ranged over the fields and forests of this new land of promise in its summer sheen,—a land watered with many rivers, and especially with that beautiful and abounding river, "the Shenandoah," which the Indians named "The Daughter of the Stars."

But prophetic as may have been the glance that saw in the fruitful valley the future home of a great and thriving people, slow were the footsteps that followed the pioneers and occupied the hunting-grounds of the receding Indians. For in those days immigration was not quickened by steam and electricity, and early tradition had pictured the transmontane country as a barren and gloomy waste, infested with serpents and wild beasts and brutal savages.

But erewhile the reports of Spotswood and his men went far and wide, and the Star of Empire beamed over the Alleghanies. And along in 1730 and 1740, we find the spray of the incoming tide breaking over the mountains—the sturdy Scotch-Irish for the most part, with some Germans and Englishmen, pouring into the Valley from Pennsylvania and Eastern Virginia, and from the fatherlands over the water. Not speculative adventurers were they, with the ambition of landlords, but bringing with them rifle and Bible, wife and child, and simple household goods—home-seekers and home-builders, who had heard of the goodly land, and who had come to stay, and who built the meeting-house and the school-house side by side when they came. Rough men were they—ready to hew their way to free and pleasant homes—but in nowise coarse men, for they were filled with high purpose, and religion and knowledge they knew should be hand-maids of each other. And showing their instinctive refinement,—where the corn waved its tassels and the wheat bowed to the wind, by their rude log huts in the wilderness there also the vine clambered, and the rose and lily bloomed.

In 1749, near Greeneville, in Augusta county—and Augusta county was then an empire stretching from the Blue Ridge mountains to the Mississippi river—in 1749 Robert Alexander, a Scotch-Irish immigrant, who was a Master of Arts of Trinity College, Dublin, established there "The Augusta Academy"—the first classical school in the Valley of Virginia. Under his successor, Rev. John Brown, the academy was first moved to "Old Providence," and again to "New Providence church," and just before the Revolution, for a third time, to Mount Pleasant, near Fairfield, in the now county of Rockbridge.

In 1776, as the revolutionary fires were kindling, there came to its head as principal William Graham, of worthy memory, who had been a class-mate and special friend of Harry Lee at Princeton College; and at the first meeting of the trustees after the battle of Lexington, while Harry Lee was donning his sword for battle, they baptized it as "Liberty Hall Academy." Another removal followed, in 1777, to near the old Timber-Ridge church; but finally, in 1785, the academy rested from its wanderings near Lexington, the little town which too had caught the flame of revolution, and was the first to take the name of that early battle-ground of the great rebellion, where

> "The embattled farmers stood
> And fired the shot heard round the world."

WASHINGTON ACADEMY AND WASHINGTON COLLEGE.

Shortly after the close of the Revolutionary war, the Legislature of Virginia, in token of esteem and admiration for the virtues and services of General George Washington, donated him one hundred shares of stock in the old James River Company. General Washington, in a characteristic manner, declined to accept the donation save only on the condition that he be permitted to appropriate it to some public purpose "in the upper part of the State," such as "the education of the children of the poor, particularly the children of such as have fallen in defence of the country." The condition granted, President Washington, in 1796—for he had then become President of the New Republic—dedicated the one hundred shares of stock "to the use of Liberty Hall Academy in Rockbridge county." Mayhap the friendship between William Graham, its principal, and his old class-mate at Princeton, "Light Horse Harry Lee," the friend of Washington, had something to do in guiding the benefaction ; but be this as it may, it was given and accepted, and in honor of the benefactor the academy was clothed with his immortal name.

In acknowledging the thanks expressed to him by the Board of Trustees, President Washington said : "To promote literature in this rising empire and to encourage the arts has ever been amongst the warmest wishes of my heart ; and if the donation which the generosity of the Legislature of the Commonwealth has enabled me to bestow upon Liberty Hall—now by your politeness called Washington Academy—is likely to prove a means to accomplish these ends, it will contribute to the gratification of my desires."

Soon after this, the Legislature, which had already incorporated the institution on a comprehensive basis, gave it the name of "The College of Washington in Virginia"—a name, however, which the trustees did not accept until 1812.* In the spirit of their beloved commander, "The Cincinnati Society," composed of survivors of the Revolutionary war, on dissolving in 1803, donated their funds, amounting to nearly $25,000, to the institution which had received his patronage and bore his name; and, thus endowed, it went forward in a career which, for nearly three-score years and ten, was a period of uninterrupted usefulness, prosperity and honor.

All ranks of honorable enterprise and ambition "in this rising empire" felt the impress of the noble spirits who came forth from its halls, trained and equipped for life's arduous tasks with keenest weapons and brightest armor. What glowing names are these that shine on the rolls of the alumni of this honored Alma Mater! Church and State, Field and Forum, Bar and Bench, Hospital and Counting-Room, Lecture-Room and Pulpit —what famous champions and teachers of the right, what trusty workers and leaders in literature and law, and arts, and arms, have they not found in her sons! Seven Governors of States— amongst them Crittenden, of Kentucky, and McDowell, Letcher, and Kemper, of Virginia; eleven United States Senators— amongst them Parker, of Virginia, Breckinridge, of Kentucky, H. S. Foote, of Mississippi, and William C. Preston, of South Carolina; more than a score of Congressmen, two-score and more of judges—amongst them Trimble, of the United States Supreme Court; Coalter, Allen, Anderson, and Burks, of the Court of Appeals of Virginia; twelve or more college presidents, and amongst them Moses Hoge and Archibald Alexander, of Hampden-Sidney, James Priestly, of Cumberland College, Tennessee; and G. A. Baxter and Henry Ruffner (who presided here), and Socrates Maupin, of the University of Virginia. These are but a few of those who here garnered the learning that shed so gracious a light in the after-time on them, their country, and their Alma Mater. And could I pause to

---

* In 1796 the Legislature of Virginia undertook to erect the Academy into a College under the name of the "College of Washington." The board of trustees resisted the enactment as an infringement of the rights of the corporation; and their grave and forcible protest was said by the late Hugh Blair Grigsby, in an address delivered in 1870, to have been the basis of the brief of Mr. Webster in the great Dartmouth College case. The act was repealed in response to this remonstrance. The name of Washington College was finally adopted in 1812.

speak of those who became valiant leaders of men in battle, I could name many a noble soldier whose eye greets mine to-day; and, alas! I should recall the form of many a hero who passed from these halls in the flush of youthful manhood, and has long slept with "the unreturning brave;" for in 1861, when the calls to arms resounded, "The Liberty-Hall Volunteers"—the students of Washington College—were among the first (and in a body) to respond; and when the quiet professor of your twin institute was baptized in history as "Stonewall Jackson," their blood o'erflowed the christening urn and reddened Manassas' field, and from Manassas to Appomattox, under Joseph E. Johnston, and Thomas J. Jackson, and Robert E. Lee, the boys and the men of Washington College proved that they were worthy of their leaders, worthy of their State and country, and worthy of all good fame.

THE FATE OF WAR.

Unsparing war spared not the shrine where breathed into the arts of peace, yet lived the spirit and was perpetuated the name of the Father of his Country. When in 1864 David Hunter led an invading army against the State from whose blood he sprung, he came not as comes the noble champion eager to strike the strong, and who realizes that he meets an equal and a generous foe. Lee had penetrated the year before to the heart of Pennsylvania, and the Southern infantry had bivouacked on the banks of the Susquehanna.

When he crossed the Pennsylvania line, he had announced in general orders, from the headquarters of the Army of Northern Virginia, that he did not come to "take vengeance;" that "we make war only upon armed men," and he therefore "earnestly exhorted the troops to abstain with most scrupulous care from unnecessary or wanton injury of private property," and "enjoined upon all officers to arrest and bring to summary punishment all who should in any way offend against the orders on the subject." He had been obeyed by his lieutenants and his men. No charred ruins, no devastated fields, no plundered homes marked the line of his march. On one occasion, to set a good example, he was seen to dismount from his horse and put up a farmer's fence. In the city of York General Early had in general orders prohibited the burning of buildings containing stores of war, lest fire might be communicated to neighboring homes; and General Gordon, in his public address, had declared: "If a torch is applied to a single dwelling, or an insult offered to a female of your town by a soldier of this command, point me out the man, and you shall have his life." The battle of Gettysburg had raged around Gettysburg College, but when it ended the college stood scathless, save by the accidents of war. But when David Hunter invaded Virginia, he came to make war on the weak and helpless, and he was as ruthless to ruin as he was swift to evade battle and to retreat. He blistered the land which he should have loved and honored, and a broad, black path marked his trail. From the summit of those mountains where Spotswood first spied the Valley, could be counted at one time the flames ascending from 118 burning houses. The Virginia Military Institute was burned, and the very statue of Washington which adorned it was carried off as a trophy. Washington College was dismantled, its scientific apparatus destroyed, its library sacked, its every apartment pillaged. The hand of war indeed fell heavily here, and when the Southern cause went down at Appomattox, Washington College remained scarce more than a ruinous and desolate relic of better days. Four professors, a handful of students, and the bare buildings, were all that was left of it.

PRESIDENT OF WASHINGTON COLLEGE.

In August, 1865, the trustees of Washington College met. The situation they contemplated was deplorable and depressing. Their invested funds were unproductive. Their treasury was empty. The State was prostrate and bankrupt. In the sky of the future there was scarcely a ray of light. But they were resolved to face difficulties and to do the best they could. One of the trustees, Colonel Bolivar Christian, of Staunton, suggested that General Lee be invited to accept the Presidency of the Institution. There was but little anticipation that he would incline to their wishes. The position could not be very remunerative,—it involved tedious and perplexing tasks, and it did not seem commensurate with the abilities, nor altogether fitting to the tastes of a great commander who had so long dealt with the vast and active concerns of military life; but the suggestion was unanimously adopted, and Hon. John W. Brockenbrough, Rector of the Board, was appointed to apprise General Lee of the fact. At first General Lee hesitated. He modestly distrusted his own competency to fulfill the trust, and he feared that the hostility of the Government towards him might direct adverse influences against the Institution which it was proposed to commit to his care. These considerations being successfully combated by those who knew how high his qualifications were, and how great were his attractions, General Lee accepted the position tendered him, and on the 2nd of October, 1865, he took the oath of office before the Rev. W. S. White—the oldest Christian minister of Lexington—and was duly installed in the presence of the trustees, professors, and students, as President of Washington College. On the eve of acceptance, two propositions were made to General Lee: one to become President of a large corporation, with a salary of $10,000 per annum; another to take the like office in another corporation, with a salary of $50,000. But he had made up his mind to come here, and this is what he said to a friend who brought him the last munificent offer:

"I have a self-imposed task which I must accomplish. I have lead the young men of the South in battle; I have seen many of them fall under my standard. I shall devote my life now to training young men to do their duty in life."

This was the high resolve that brought him here, and Robert E. Lee seemed to be the great, heroic Captain when he stood before the Virginia Convention with superb courage and dauntless mien, and "devoted his sword to his native State," he seemed informed with a spirit that gathered its strength and loveliness from Heaven, when he stood here and consecrated his remaining years to training up to life's duties, the sons, brothers and comrades of those who had followed him in battle. Young men of the South! to him who thus stood by us, we owe a debt immeasurable, and as long as our race is upon earth, let our children and our children's childen hold that debt sacred.

GENERAL LEE'S ADMINISTRATION AS COLLEGE PRESIDENT.

General Lee was eminently qualified for the task assumed. His own education had been liberal and thorough. In his youth he had been grounded by his tutors in a knowledge of ancient history, and of the dead languages, the Latin and the Greek, and the tastes thus early stimulated had been preserved and cultivated in after years. As a cadet at West Point he graduated second in a distinguished class, excellence of conduct and excellence of attainment going hand in hand. Appointed an officer of Engineers when he entered the army, and often charged with most important works, the duties devolved upon him required assiduous study and research. Still later, after he returned with great distinction from Mexico, he became the Superintendent and Head of the Military Academy at West Point, and occupying that position for three years, he acquired experience and developed capacities which singularly fitted him for the sphere which he now entered—the training of youth. It is indicative of his comprehensive views of education, that during his superintendency at West Point, the course of study was extended to five years and greatly enlarged in its scope. And when he entered upon his duties here, it was soon evident that he possessed every qualification to direct with signal success, the affairs of the Institution, and to mould the characters and minds of those confided to his care.

It was understood from the time of his inauguration that he would not himself act as teacher of any class; but would have in charge the business and financial concerns of the College—its educational curriculum, and the discipline of its students; and from first to last, he devoted himself to these tasks with unceasing assiduity and success.

Everything here felt with his presence a renovating and progressive impulse. Nothing escaped his attention, from the smallest detail of business to the gravest question of educational policy; and in whatever concerned the well-being of the College, its Faculty and its students, his discerning judgment and his sympathetic heart worked out the right result. Under his supervision the buildings were repaired, the accommodations enlarged, the chemical and philosophical apparatus replaced, the library replenished and reformed. He it was who selected the site of yon Chapel which now guard his mortal remains—his was the hand that draughted the plan, and his the eye that saw its parts conjoined together. No figure-head was he, but a worker, and doer, bringing things to pass as they should be.

Prior to his administration, there were but five Chairs of Instruction, several Departments being combined under one professional head:

1. Mental and Moral Science, and political economy.
2. Latin Language and Literature.
3. Greek Language and Literature.
4. Mathematics and Physical Science.
5. Chemistry and Natural Philosophy.

Speedily after his accession, three new Chairs were added, and Professors elected to fill them; the Chair of Natural Philosophy, embracing, in addition to physics, Acoustics, Optics, &c., the various subjects of Natural and Applied Mechanics; the Chair of Applied Mathematics, embracing Astronomy, Civil and Military Engineering; and Chair of Modern Languages, to which was added English Philosophy. In the second year of his incumbency the Chair of History and English Literature was established, and soon afterwards the department of "Law and Equity," under that eminent jurist, Judge John W. Brockenbrough.

Several other Chairs were included in the President's programme, one of the "English Language," one of "Applied Chemistry," and also, " A School of Medicine," a " School of Journalism " and a " School of Commerce "—the latter being designed to give special instruction and systematic training in whatever pertained to business in the most enlarged sense of the term. Amongst other changes introduced by General Lee was the substitution of the elective system instead of a fixed curriculum; and the system of discipline which he adopted, in no wise partaking of the military type, to which it might have been supposed his disposition would incline—was that which has so long prospered at the University of Virginia; a system which ignored espionage and compulsion, and put every student upon a manly sense of honor—a system which, especially with young men not too immature to appreciate it, and which, with all men who have the capacity of being gentlemen, is the best calculated to develop the virtuous and independent elements of character. Here for five years the General devoted himself to the cause of education, and here under him that cause nobly flourished. Here he demonstrated that comprehensive grasp of every subject connected with his sphere; and the keen appehension of the demands of this progressive age, and of a land entering as it were upon a new birth. His associates in the Faculty loved him as a father, and all who saw or knew his work, with common voice proclaimed the conviction expressed by one of the most distinguished of his associates, that he was " the best College President that this country has ever produced."

His work has been established, and though the great Chief has "fallen by the way," one who bears his name, and who is worthy of it, has taken up the lines that fell from his hands; and under him, with God's blessing, the good cause goes on prospering and to prosper.

And so happily it has come to pass that the little school of the pioneers, planted in the wilderness, is to-day a great university; that the ambition of William Graham, the college mate of Henry Lee, has been realized beyond its sweetest dream; that the college which the Father of his Country lifted up by his generosity from a struggling academy to educate the children of those who had fallen in its defense; and which was blighted to the verge of destruction, has been restored and magnified by the hand of him who alone of all men, living or dead, now equally shares with his illustrious prototype, the eulogy pronounced by his own sire, Light Horse Harry Lee:

"*First in Peace, first in War, and first in the hearts of his Countrymen.*"

LEE THE MAN—HIS PERSONAL APPEARANCE.

Thus feebly and imperfectly have I attempted to trace the military achievements and services of him to whose memory this day is dedicated. Lee the General, stands abreast with the greatest captains of all time, and Lee the Patriot, has universal homage. It is now of Lee the Man, that I would speak:

In personal appearance, General Lee was a man whom once to see was ever to remember. His figure was tall, erect, well proportioned, lithe and graceful. A fine head, with broad, uplifted brow, and features boldly but yet delicately chiseled, bore the high aspect of one born to command. The firm yet mobile lips, and the thick-set jaw, were expressive of daring and resolution; and the dark scintillant eye flashed with the light of a brilliant intellect and a fearless spirit. His whole countenance, indeed, bespoke alike a powerful mind, and indomitable will, yet beamed with charity, gentleness and benevolence. In his manners, quiet, reserve, unaffected courtesy and native dignity, made manifest the character of one who can only be described by the name of gentleman. And taken all in all, his presence possessed that grave and simple majesty which commanded instant reverence and repressed familiarity; and yet so charmed by a certain modesty and gracious deference, that reverence and confidence were ever ready to kindle into affection. It was impossible to look upon him, and not to recognize at a glance that in him, nature gave assurance of a man created great and good.

Mounted in the field, and at the head of his troops, a glimpse of Lee was an inspiration. His figure was as distinctive as that of Napoleon. Ah! soldiers! who can forget it? The black slouch hat, the cavalry boots, the dark cape, the plain gray coat without an ornament but the three stars on the collar, the calm, victorious face, the splendid, manly figure on the gray warhorse, that steps as if proudly conscious of his rider; he looked every inch the true knight—the grand, invincible champion of a great principle.

MENTAL ATTRIBUTES AND ATTAINMENTS.

The intellectual abilities of General Lee were of the highest order, and his attainments, scientific and literary, were remarkable for one who had devoted so many years of his life to the exacting duties and details of the camp and the field. He read much, digested what he read, and amplified his readings with reflective power. But so modest and unpretentious was he—so chastened and retiring was his ambition, and his overshadowing military exploits had so fixed the admiring gaze of men, that when he came here few knew how rare were the accomplishments, and how versatile and adaptive was the genius of the gentleman who seemed by nature framed to lead the ranks and grace the habiliments of war. The training, habits and occupations of the soldier seldom guide his footsteps to classic haunts, and when the great Captain is unhorsed and his trappings disappear, how often do we find that the soldier was a soldier only, and nothing more. But when Lee the soldier stepped forth in civic dress, it was soon evident to all, as it had been previously to those who knew him best, that here was one full panoplied to dignify and adorn any civic station ; one who disclosed himself in wide converse and correspondence embracing all manner of delicate and difficult situations, to possess that quality which is the consummate flower of wisdom—*unerring judgment combined with exquisite taste.* The literature that may be found in the letters of the great, unfolds the very essence of the genius of the men and of the times they lived in ; and in my humble judgment it were sufficient to read the letters written by General Lee, and which are collated in the beautiful memorial volume* prepared by Rev. Dr. J. Wm. Jones, to discern that the writer was one who profoundly comprehended the topics of the day, and wielded a pen as vigorous and polished as his sword. And when we contemplate in connection with his deeds the fair and lofty character that is

---

* "Personal Reminiscences, Anecdotes and Letters of General R. E. Lee," by J. Wm. Jones, Secretary Southern Historical Society.

mirrored in them, we behold one whose strong, equitable and wide-reaching mind was such that had he devoted it to jurisprudence, had made the name of Justice as venerable and august as when a Marshall enunciated the law; who, had he been a statesman, had moulded the institutions of his country, and guided its political currents with as wise, firm and temperate a hand as that of Washington; who, had he headed any of the great corporate enterprises of transportation, commerce or development in which aggregated capital relies on scientific sagacity for great works, had greatly aided the solution of many perplexing problems that now agitate the public mind; who, had he bent himself to literature, had produced a page filled with the glory and dignity of philosophic inquiry or historic truth—one indeed so perfectly balanced in mind and will, so nobly turned in moral worth, so just in heart, so clear in thought, and so authoritative in direction that in any land where the common sentiment can have spontaneous play, would, as inevitably as the sparks fly upward, and by a law scarce less fixed than that which moves the planets in their course, have been the leading man in whatever he undertook, and would have been called by one voice to become the Chief Magistrate of the people.

TRUE HEROISM—THE HEROISM OF LEE.

As little things make up the sum of life, so they reveal the inward nature of men and furnish keys to history. It is in the office, the street, the field, the workshop, and by the fireside, that men show what stuff they are made of, not less than in those eventful actions which write themselves in lightnings across the skies and mark the rise and fall of nations. Nay, more—the highest attributes of human nature are not disclosed in action, but in self-restraint and repose. "Self-restraint," as has been truly said by Thomas Hughes, "is the highest form of self-assertion."

It is harder, as every soldier knows, to lie down and take the fire of batteries without returning it, than to rise and charge to the cannon's mouth. It is harder to give the soft answer that turns away wrath than to retort a word with a blow. De Long, in the frozen Arctic wastes, dying alone inch by inch of cold and starvation, yet intent on his work, and writing lines for the benefit of others, deserved, as well as the Marshal of France who received it, the name of " bravest of the brave." The artless little Alabama girl, who was guiding General Forrest along a dangerous path when the enemy fired a volley upon him, and who instinctively spread her skirts and cried : " Get behind me !" had a spirit as high as that which filled the bosom of Joan of Arc or Charlotte Corday.

The little Holland boy, who, seeing the water oozing through the dyke, and the town near by about to be deluged and destroyed, neither cried nor ran, but stopped, and all alone, stifled the opening gap with earth, in instant peril of being swept to death unhonored and unknown, showed a finer and nobler fibre than that of Cambronne when he shouted to the conquering British : " The Guard dies, but never surrenders." The soldier of Pompeii, buried at his post standing there, and flying not from the hot waves of lava that rolled over him, tells the Roman story in grander language than the ruins of the Coliseum. And Herndon, on the deck of his ship, doing all to save his passengers, making deliberate choice of death before dishonor, and going down into the great deep with brow calm and unruffled, is a grander picture of true, heroic temper than that of Cæsar leading his legions, or of the young Corsican at the Bridge of Lodi.

Amongst the quiet, nameless workers of the world—in the stubble field and by the forge, bending over a sick child's bed or smoothing an outcast's pillow, is many a hero and heroine truer, nobler than those over whose brows hang plumes and laurels.

In action there is the stimulus of excited physical faculties, and of the moving passions—but in the composure of the calm mind that quietly devotes itself to hard life-work—putting aside temptations—contemplating and rising superior to all surroundings of adversity, suffering, danger and death, man is revealed in his highest manifestation. Then, and then alone, he seems to have redeemed his fallen state, and to be recreated in God's image. At the bottom of all true heroism is unselfishness. Its crowning expression is sacrifice. The world is suspicious of vaunted heroes. They are so easily manufactured. So many feet are cut and trimmed to fit Cinderella's slippers that we hesitate long before we hail the Princess. But when the true Hero has come, and we know that here he is, in verity, Ah! how the hearts of men leap forth to greet him—how worshipfully we welcome God's noblest work—the strong, honest, fearless, upright man.

In Robert Lee was such a hero vouchsafed to us and to mankind, and whether we behold him declining command of the Federal army to fight the battles and share the miseries of his own people; proclaiming on the heights in front of Gettysburg that the fault of the disaster was his own; leading charges in the crisis of combat; walking under the yoke of conquest without a murmur of complaint; or refusing fortunes to come here and train the youth of his country in the path of duty—he is ever the same meek, grand, self-sacrificing spirit. Here he exhibited qualities not less worthy and heroic than those displayed on the broad and open theatre of conflict, when the eyes of nations watched his every action. Here in the calm repose of civil and domestic duties, and in the trying routine of incessant tasks, he lived a life as high as when, day by day, he marshalled and led his thin and wasting lines, and slept by night upon the field that was to be drenched again in blood upon the morrow.

Here in these quiet walks, far removed from "war or battle's sound," came into view, as when the storm o'er past the mountain seems a pinnacle of light, the landscape beams with fresher and tenderer beauties, and the purple, golden clouds float above us in the azure depths like the Islands of the Blest, so came into view the towering grandeur, the massive splendor and the loving kindness of the character of General Lee, and the very sorrows that overhung his life seemed luminous with celestial hues. Here he revealed in manifold gracious hospitalities, tender charities, and patient, worthy counsels, how deep and pure and inexhaustible were the fountains of his virtues. And loving hearts delight to recall, as loving lips will ever delight to tell, the thousand little things he did which sent forth lines of light to irradiate the gloom of the conquered land, and to lift up the hopes and cheer the works of the people.

Was there a scheme of public improvement? He took hearty interest in promoting its success in every way he could. Was there an enterprise of charity, or education, or religion, that needed friendly aid? He gave it according to his store, and sent with the gift words that were deeds. Was there a poor soldier in distress? Whoever else forgot him, it was not Lee. Was there a proud spirit chafing under defeat, and breaking forth in angry complaints and criminations, or a wanderer who had sought in other lands an unvexed retreat denied him here? He it was who with mild voice conjured restraint and patience, recalled the wanderer home and reared above the desolate hearthstone the image of duty. And whosoever mourned the loved and lost, who had died in vain for the cause now perished, he it was who poured into the stricken heart the balm of sympathy and consolation.

Here, indeed, Lee, no longer the Leader, became, as it were, the Priest of his people, and the young men of Washington College were but a fragment of those who found in his voice and his example the shining signs that never misguided their footsteps.

INCIDENTS OF HIS LIFE AND ILLUSTRATIONS OF HIS CHARACTER.

Many are the illustrations and incidents which show how beautifully blended in his character were the sterner qualities that command respect, with the gentle traits that engage affection. And his quick apprehension of every natural beauty, and keen sympathy, for all living things show the exquisite sensibilities of his heart. His letters from Mexico teem with expressions of the delight with which he looked upon the bright-winged birds and luxuriant flowers of that sunny land, and during the Confederate war, when cramped resources denied bestowal of the smallest tokens of friendship, we find his letters to dear ones frequently laden with the floral emblems of his constant thought and love. In one of them he says: "I send you some sweet violets that I gathered for you this morning while covered with the dense white frost whose crystals glittered in the bright sun like diamonds, and formed a brooch of rare beauty and sweetness which could not be fabricated by the expenditure of a world of money."

And when after the war he visited Alexandria, the scene of his boyhood days, one of his old neighbors found him gazing over the palings of the garden where he used to play. "I am looking," he said, "to see if the old snow-ball trees are still here. I should be sorry to miss them." How he loved, too, these grand mountains! Amongst them, mounted on his faithful war-horse, Traveller, he often roamed while he spent his days amongst you. And here in nature's works he found refreshment from the toils of life, and looked from nature up to nature's God.

His tenderness was as instinctive as his valor. A writer who, on one occasion, stood in his company watching a fire in the mountains, relates how, when others were wrapt in its scenic grandeur, General Lee remarked: "It is beautiful! but I have been thinking of the poor animals that must perish in the flames." And another tells how, when in the lines near Richmond, the bolts of battle swept the point where the General stood, he ordered his attendants to the rear, and while himself calmly surveying the field under fire, he stopped to pick up a fledging sparrow that had fallen from its nest, and restore it to the bough overhead.

Pictures, are these, full of infinite suggestion!

A Robespierre and a Torquemada may exhibit emotional tenderness, shallow and fitful, but that of Lee was the vital principle of a robust, exalted nature, which found its inspirations in the sacred heart of Charity, and diffused itself in ceaseless acts of magnanimity and love.

So it was that while the passions of men were loosened, and the fierce work of war spread havoc and desolation far and wide, he who directed its tremendous forces with stern and nervous hand, moved also amongst its scenes of woe—a gracious and healing spirit. So it was to him a stricken foe was a foe no longer—that his orders to the surgeons of his army were to "treat the whole field alike," and when, at Chancellorsville, he in person led the tempestuous assault that won the victory, and stood amongst the wounded of the blue and gray, heaped around him in indiscriminate carnage—his first thought and care were for them, alike in their common suffering. So it was that whether in Pennsylvania, Maryland, or Virginia, he restrained every excess of conduct, and held the reckless and the ruthless within those bounds which duty sets to action. So it was that to one homeless during the days of strife, he wrote: "Occupy yourself in helping those more helpless than yourself." So it was, that when the gallant General Phil. Kearney fell at Ox Hill, he sent his sword and horse through the lines to his mourning widow—and that when Lincoln was struck down by an assassin's hand, he denounced the deed as " a crime previously unknown to the country, and one that must be deprecated by every American." And so, too, when one day here, a man humbly clad sought alms at his door, Lee pointed to his retiring form and said: " That is one of our old soldiers who is in necessitous circumstances. He fought on the other side, but we must not remember that against him now." And this poor soldier said of him afterwards: " He is the noblest man that ever lived. He not only had a kind word for me, but he gave me some money to help me on my way." Better is that praise than any garland of the Poet or the Rhetorician.

THE RELATIONS BETWEEN LEE AND HIS MEN.

As we glance back through the smoke-drifts of his many campaigns and battles, his kind, considerate acts towards his officers and men gleam through them as brightly as their burnished weapons; and they formed a fellowship as noble as that which bound the Knights of the Round Table to Arthur, " the blameless King." His principle of discipline was indicated in his expression that " a true man of honor feels himself humbled when he cannot help humbling others," and never exercising stern authority except when absolutely indispensable, his influence was the more potent because it ever appealed to honorable motives and natural affections. In the dark days of the Revolution, two Major-Generals conspired with a faction of the Continental Congress to put Gates in the place of Washington, denominating him a "weak General." Never did Confederate dream a disloyal thought of Lee, and the greater the disaster, the more his army leaned upon him.

When Jackson fell, Lee wrote to him: " You are better off than I am, for while you have lost your left arm, I have lost my right arm." And Jackson said of him: "Lee is a phenomenon. He is the only man that I would follow blindfold." Midway between Petersburg and Appomattox, with the ruins of an Empire falling on his shoulders, and the gory remnants of his army staggering under the thick blows of the advancing foe, we see Lee turning aside from the column, and riding up to the home of the widow of the gallant Colonel John Thornton, who had fallen at Sharpsburg. " I have not time to tarry," he says, " but I could not pass by without stopping a moment to pay my respects to the widow of my honored soldier, Colonel Thorton, and tender her my deepest sympathy in the sore bereavement she sustained when the country was deprived of his invaluable services."

Three of his sons were there in the army with him; but they were too noble to seek, and he too noble to bestow, honors because of the tie of blood. One of them, a private in the artillery, served his gun with his fellows. Another is in a hostile prison, and a Federal officer of equal rank begs that General Lee will effect an exchange, the one for the other. The General declined, saying, "that he will ask no favor for his own son that could not be asked for the humblest private in the army." On the cars, crowded with passengers, a soldier, scarce noticed, struggles to draw his coat over his wounded arm. One from amongst many rises and goes to his aid. It is General Lee. An army surgeon relates that while the battle of the Crater raged, General Lee rode to the rear of the line where the wounded lay, and, dismounting, moved amongst them. " Doctor, why are you not doing something for this man," he said, pointing to one sorely stricken. The Doctor raised the gray jacket and pointed to the ghastly wound which made life hopeless. General Lee bent tenderly over the wounded man and then in a voice tremulous with emotion, exclaimed : " Alas! poor soldier! may God make soft his dying pillow."

Such were some of the many acts that made the men love Lee. And in the fight he was ever ready to be foremost. Lee the Soldier, over-rode Lee the General, and when the pinch and struggle came, there was he. "Lee to the rear" became the soldiers' battle-cry ; and oftentimes, when the long lines came gleaming on, and shot and shell in tempest ripped the earth, uptore the forest and filled the air with death, those soldiers in their rusty rags, paused as they saw his face amongst them ; and then, with manhood's imperious love, these sovereigns of the field commanded, "General Lee, go back," as their condition of advancing. And then forward to the death. Was ever such devotion? Yes, Lee loved his men " as a father pitieth his children," and they loved him with a love that "passeth the love of woman," for they saw in him the iron hero who could lead the brave with front as dauntless as a warrior's crest, and the gentle friend who comforted the stricken with soul as tender as a mother's prayer.

FORGIVENESS.

Lee had nothing in common with the little minds that know not how to forgive. His was the land that had been invaded ; his the people who were cut down, ravaged and ruined ; his the home that was torn away and spoliated ; his was the cause that perished. He was the General discrowned of his mighty place, and he the citizen disfranchised. Yet Lee forgave, and counselled all to forgive and forget.

The Greek poet has said :

> "The firmest mind will fail
> Beneath misfortune's stroke, and stunned, depart
> From its sage plan of action."

But the mind of Lee received the rude shock of destiny without a quiver; so the genial currents of his sweet, heroic soul rolled on unruffled, while in their calm, pure depths were reflected the light of heaven.

When a minister once denounced the North, and the indictment of General Lee for treason, the general followed him to the door and said: "Doctor, there is a good old book which I read, and you preach from, which says: 'Love your enemies, bless them that curse you, do good to them that hate you, and pray for them which dispitefully use you.' Do you think your remarks this evening were quite in the spirit of that teaching?" And he added: "I have fought against the people of the North because I believed they were seeking to wrest from the South her dearest rights. But I have never cherished toward them bitter or vindictive feelings, and have never seen the day when I did not pray for them."

Soon after the passage of those harsh acts of Congress, disfranchising Confederates for participating in the war, and while every Southern breast was filled with indignation, some friends in General Lee's presence expressed themselves with great bitterness. The General turned to the table near him, where lay the manuscript of his father's life, which he was then editing, and read these lines:

> "Learn from yon Orient shell to love thy foe,
> And store with pearls the hand that brings thee woe;
> Free like yon rock, from base, vindictive pride,
> Emblaze with gems the wrist that rends thy side
> Mark where yon tree rewards the stony shower,
> With fruit nectarious or the balmy flower;
> All Nature cries aloud: shall men do less
> Than love the smiter, and the railer bless?"

"These lines," said he, "were written in Arabia, and by a Mahomedan, the Poet of Shiraz, the immortal Hafiz; and ought not we, who profess to be governed by the principles of Christianity, to rise at least to the standard of this Mahomedan poet, and learn to forgive our enemies?"

In the rush of this age, a character so simply meek and so proudly, grandly strong, is scarce comprehensible to the eager, restless competitors for wealth and place and power. And the "practical man," as he is called, who ever keeps a keen eye to the main chance, and is esteemed happy just in proportion as fortune favors his schemes of ambition or profit, is apt to attribute weakness to one so void of self-seeking and resentment, and so amiable and gentle in his feelings and conduct towards his fellow-men. But could he have seen with what patient attention to detail this ceaseless worker dispatched business and brought great results from small materials—with what quick, strong, comprehensive grasp he solved difficulties and conquered dangers - what good cheer he gave the toiling: what hope he gave the despondent : what comfort he gave the afflicted. Aye! could he have caught the glance of that eagle eye, and looked on that serene, bold brow which over-awed the field of battle. and then beheld the swift, stern, inspiring energy which propelled its forces to deeds which seemed almost impossible to man—there would have been to him a new revelation. He would have beheld a character which, to one unacquainted with it, would seem to have been idealized by the genius of the poet rather that to have existed in the flesh, and to have stepped forth from the sanctuary of romance rather than to have belonged to real history. He would have realized, by contact with this simple gentleman, that the true greatness and true glory of man lies in those elements which are superior to fortune—that he is most practical who is himself above it, and that happiness, if ever on earth happiness be found, has fixed her temple only in the heart that is without guile, and is without reproach of man or woman.

THE LAST DAYS OF GENERAL LEE.

Five years rolled by while here " the self-imposed mission " of Lee was being accomplished, and now, in 1870, he had reached the age of sixty-three. A robust constitution, never abused by injurious habits, would doubtless have prolonged his life beyond the three-score years and ten which the Psalmist has ascribed as the allotted term of man ; but many causes were sapping and undermining it. The exposures of two wars in which he had participated, and the tremendous strain on nerves and heart and brain which his vast responsibilities and his accumulated trials had entailed, had been silently and gradually doing their work; and now his step had lost something of its elasticity, the shoulders began to stoop as if under a growing burden, and the ruddy glow of health upon his countenance had passed into a feverish flush. Into his ears, and into his heart, had been poured the afflictions of his people, and while composed and self-contained and uncomplaining, who could have looked upon that great face, over whose majestic lineaments there stole the shade of sadness, without perceiving that grief for those he loved was gnawing at the heart strings? without perceiving in the brilliant eye, which now and then had a far-away, abstracted gaze, that the soul within bore a sorrow " that only Heaven could heal."

What he suffered his lips have never spoken. In the beautiful language of another : " His lips were closed like the gates of some majestic temple, not for concealment, but because that within was holy." Yet, let us take consolation to ourselves that there came to him much to give him joy. Around him were those united by the closest ties of blood and relationship in unremitting fidelity. Not a man of those who ever fought under him—aye, not one—ever proved faithless in respect for him; the great mass of them gave to him every expression in their power of their affection. To the noble mind, sweet is the generous and genuine praise of noble men, and for Lee there was full measure. He lived to see deeply laid the foundation, and firmly built the pedestal, of his great glory, and to catch the murmur of those voices which would rear high his image and bear his name and fame to remote ages, and distant nations. The brave and true of every land paid him tribute. The first soldiers of foreign climes saluted him with eulogy; the scholar decorated his page with dedication to his name, the artist enshrined his form and features in noblest work of brush and chisel, the poet hymned the heroic pathos of his life in tender, lofty strain. Enmity grew into friendship before his noble bearing, and humanity itself attended him with all human sympathy. And over all, " God made soft his dying pillow."

DEATH.

The particular form of his mortal malady was rheumatism of the heart, originating in the exposure of his campaigns, and aggravated by the circumstances of his many trying situations. He traveled South in the spring of 1870, and in the summer resorted to the Hot Springs of Virginia; and when September came, he was here in better health and spirits, at his accustomed work. On the 28th of September, he conducted, as usual, his correspondence, and performed the incidental tasks of his office, and after dinner he attended a meeting of the Vestry of Grace Episcopal Church, of which body he was a member. A question as to the minister's salary coming before the Board, and there being a deficiency in the amount necessary, General Lee said: "I will give that sum." A sense of weariness came over him before the meeting ended, and at its close he retired with wan, flushed face. Returning home, he found the family circle gathered for tea, and took his place at the board, standing to say grace. The lips failed to voice the blessings prompted by the heart, and without a word he took his seat with an expression of sublime resignation on his face; for well he knew that the Master's call had come, and he was ready to answer.

He was borne to his chamber, and skilled physicians and loving hands did all that man could do. For nearly a fortnight

"Twixt night and morn upon the horizon's verge,
Between two worlds life hovered like a star."

And thus on the morning of October 12th, the star of the mortal sank into the sunrise of immortality, and Robert Lee passed hence to "where beyond these voices there is peace."

"Tell A. P. Hill to prepare for action," were amongst the last words of Stonewall Jackson. "Tell Hill he *must* come up," were the last words of Lee. Their brave Lieutenant, who rests under the green turf of Hollywood, seems to have been latest in the minds of his great commanders, while their spirits yet in martial fancy, roamed again the fields of conflict, and ere they passed to where the soldier dreams of battle-fields no more.

THE LESSONS OF HIS LIFE.

And did he live in vain, this brave and gentle Lee? And have his works perished with him? I would blush to ask the question save to give the answer.

A leader of armies he closed his career in complete disaster. But the military scientist studies his campaigns, and finds in them designs as bold and brilliant and actions as intense and energetic as ever illustrated the art of war. The gallant captain beholds in his bearing, courage as rare as ever forced a desperate field, or restored a lost one. The private soldier looks up at an image as benignant and commanding as ever thrilled the heart with highest impulse of devotion.

The men who wrested victory from his little band, stood wonder-stricken and abashed when they saw how few were those who dared oppose them, and generous admiration burst into spontaneous tribute to the splendid leader who bore defeat with the quiet resignation of a hero. The men who fought under him never revered or loved him more than on the day he sheathed his sword. Had he but said the word, they would have died for honor. It was because he said the word that they resolved to live for duty.

Plato congratulated himself, first, that he was born a man; second, that he had the happiness of being a Greek; and, third, that he was the contemporary of Sophocles. And in this vast throng to-day, and here and there the wide world over, is many an one who wore the grey, who rejoices that he was born a man to do a man's part for his suffering country; that he had the glory of being a Confederate; and who feels a just, proud and glowing consciousness in his bosom when he says unto himself: "I was a follower of Robert Lee. I was a soldier in the army of Northern Virginia."

DID HE WIELD PATRONAGE AND POWER?

No, he could not have appointed a friend to the smallest office. He could bestow no emolument upon any of his followers. But an intimation of his wish amongst his own people carried an influence which the command of the autocrat can never possess, and his approval of conduct or character was deemed an honor, and was an honor, which outvied the stars and crosses and titles conferred by kings.

DID HE GAIN WEALTH.

No. He neither sought nor despised it. It thrust itself upon him, but he put it away from him. He refused its companionship because its people could not have its company. He gave what he had to a weak cause, and to those whose necessities were greater than his own. And home itself he sacrificed on the altar of his country. But he refuted the shallow worldling's maxim that "every man has his price," and proved that true manhood has none, however great.

The plunderer of India defended himself by exclaiming that "when he considered his opportunities, he was astonished at his own moderation." Mark Antony appeased the anger of the Roman populace against the fallen tyrant by Cæsar's will, wherein he left them his rich and fair possessions—to them and their heirs forever. The Captive of St. Helena, aggrandized with the tears and blood of Europe, drew his own long will, dispensing millions to his favorites. Lee had opportunities as great as any conqueror and took nothing—not even that which others pushed upon him.

But he has left a great, imperishable legacy to us and our heirs forever. The heart of man is his perpetual kingdom. There he reigns transcendent, and we exclaim: "Oh, king, live forever."

DID HE POSSESS RANK?

Not so. Far from it. He was not even a citizen. The country which gave the right of suffrage to the alien ere he could speak its language, and to the African freedman ere he could read or understand its laws, denied to him the privilege of a ballot. He had asked amnesty. He had been refused. He had not been tried, but he had been convicted. He forgave, but he was unforgiven. He died a paroled prisoner of war, in the calm of peace, five years after war had ended—died the foremost and noblest man in a Republic which proclaims itself "the land of the free and the home of the brave," himself and his Commander-in-Chief constituting the most conspicuous of its political slaves. But as the oak, stripped of the foliage by the winter blast, then, and then only, stands forth in solemn and mighty majesty against the wintry sky, so Robert Lee, stripped of every rank that man could give him, towered above the earth and those around him, in the pure sublimity and strength of that character which we can only fitly contemplate when we lift our eyes from earth and see it dimmed against the Heavens!

DID HE SAVE HIS COUNTRY FROM CONQUEST?

No. He saw his every foreboding of evil verified. He came to share the miseries of his people. He shared them, drinking every drop of Sorrow's cup. His cause was lost, and the land for which he fought lives not amongst the nations. But the voice of History echoes the poet's song:

> "Ah! realm of tombs! but let it bear
> This blazon to the last of times;
> No nation rose so white and fair,
> Or fell so pure from crimes."

And he, its type, lived and died, teaching life's greatest lessons, "to suffer and be strong," and that "misfortune nobly borne is good fortune."

There is a rare exotic that blooms but once in a century, and then it fills the light with beauty and the air with fragrance. In each of the two centuries of Virginia's Statehood, there has sprung from the loins of her heroic race, a son whose name and deeds will bloom throughout the ages. Each fought for Liberty and Independence; each against a people of his own race; each against the forms of established power. George Washington won against a kingdom whose seat was three thousand miles away, whose soldiers had to sail in ships across the deep, and he found in the boundless areas of his own land its strongest fortifications. August, beyond the reach of detraction, is the glory of his name. Robert Edward Lee made fiercer and bloodier fight against greater odds, and at greater sacrifice, and lost—against the greatest nation of modern history, armed with steam and electricity, and all the appliances of modern science; a nation which mustered its hosts at the very threshold of his door. But his life teaches the grandest lesson how manhood can rise transcendent over Adversity, and is in itself alone, under God, pre-eminent—the grander lesson, because as sorrow and misfortune are sooner or later the common lot—even that of him who is to-day the conqueror—he who bears them best is made of sterner stuff, and is the most useful and universal, as he is the greatest and noblest exemplar.

And now he has vanished from us forever. And is this all that is left of him—this handful of dust beneath the marble stone? No, the Ages answer as they rise from the gulfs of Time, where lay the wrecks of kingdoms and estates, holding up in their hands as their only trophies, the names of those who have wrought for man in the love and fear of God, and in love unfearing for their fellow-men.

No! the present answers, bending by his tomb.

No! the future answers, as the breath of the morning fans its radiant brow, and its soul drinks in sweet inspirations from the lovely life of Lee.

No, methinks the very heavens echo, as melt into their depths the words of reverent love that voice the hearts of men to the tingling stars.

CONCLUSION.

Come we then to-day in loyal love to sanctify our memories, to purify our hopes, to make strong all good intent by communion with the spirit of him, who, being dead, yet speaketh. Come, child, in thy spotless innocence ; come, woman, in thy purity ; come, youth, in thy prime ; come, manhood, in thy strength ; come, age, in thy ripe wisdom ; come citizen, come soldier, let us strew the roses and lilies of June around his tomb, for he, like them, exhaled in his life Nature's beneficence, and the grave has consecrated that life, and given it to us all; let us crown his tomb with the oak, the emblem of his strength, and with the laurel, the emblem of his glory, and let these guns, whose voices he knew of old, awake the echoes of the mountains that Nature herself may join in his solemn requiem.

Come, for here he rests, and—

> ' On this green bank, by this fair stream,
> We set to-day a native stone,
> That memory may his deeds redeem,
> When, like our sires, our sons are gone."

Come, for here the genius of loftiest poesy in the artist's dream, and through the sculptor's touch, has restored his form and features—a Valentine has lifted the marble veil and disclosed him to us as we would love to look upon him—lying, the flower of knighthood, in "Joyous Gard." His sword beside him is sheathed forever. But honor's seal is on his brow, and valor's star is on his breast, and the peace that passeth all understanding descends upon him. Here, not in the hour of his grandest triumph of earth, as when mid the battle roar, shouting battalions followed his trenchant sword, and bleeding veterans forgot their wounds to leap between him and his enemies—but here in victory, supreme over earth itself, and over death, its conqueror, he rests, his warfare done.

And as we seem to gaze once more on him we loved and hailed as chief, in his sweet, dreamless sleep, the tranquil face is clothed with heaven's light, and the mute lips seem eloquent with the message that in life he spoke:

" *There is a true glory and a true honor ; the glory of duty done, the honor of the integrity of principle.*"

After the conclusion of Major Daniel's oration, Father Ryan, at the request of Gen. Early, recited his celebrated poem:

THE SWORD OF LEE.

Forth from its scabbard, pure and bright,
    Flashed the sword of Lee !
Far in the front of the deadly fight,
High o'er the brave in the cause of right,
Its stainless sheen, like a beacon-light,
    Led us to victory.

Out of its scabbard, where full long,
    It slumbered peacefully—
Roused from its rest by the battle-song,
Shielding the feeble, smiting the strong,
Guarding the right, and avenging the wrong
    Gleamed the sword of Lee !

Forth from its scabbard, high in air,
    Beneath Virginia's sky—
And they who saw it gleaming there,
And knew who bore it, knelt to swear
That where that sword led they would dare
    To follow and to die.

Out of its scabbard! Never hand
    Waved sword from stain as free,
Nor purer sword led braver band,
Nor braver bled for a brighter land,
Nor brighter land had a cause as grand,
    Nor cause, a chief like Lee !

Forth from its scabbard ! how we prayed
    That sword might victor be !
And when our triumph was delayed,
And many a heart grew sore afraid,
We still hoped on, while gleamed the blade
    Of noble Robert Lee !

Forth from its scabbard ! all in vain !
    Forth flashed the sword of Lee !
'Tis shrouded now in its sheath again,
It sleeps the sleep of our noble slain,
Defeated, yet without a stain,
    Proudly and peacefully.

www.ingramcontent.com/pod-product-compliance
Lightning Source LLC
Chambersburg PA
CBHW020323090426
42735CB00009B/1378